D0191274

EDWARD R. MURROW'S

This I Believe®

SELECTIONS FROM THE 1950s

RADIO SERIES

EDWARD R. MURROW'S

This I Believe®

SELECTIONS FROM THE 1950s

RADIO SERIES

EDITED BY

Dan Gediman

WITH John Gregory AND Mary Jo Gediman

EDITORIAL TEAM OF THE 1950s SERIES

Gladys Chang Hardy, Reny Hill, Donald J. Merwin,
Edward P. Morgan, Edward R. Murrow, Raymond Swing,
and Ward Wheelock

Edward R. Murrow's This I believe: selections from the 1950s radio series / edited by
Dan Gediman; with John Gregory and Mary Jo Gediman.

ISBN-13: 978-1-4196-8040-3
ISBN-10: 1-4196-8040-4

Designed by Chris Enander, TBD Design, Louisville, Kentucky

To Margot Trevor Wheelock, who was responsible

for This I Believe

Contents

Contents

CONTENTS

Contents

Contents

Foreword

⁓

Dan Gediman

It was March 2003. I was home sick with the flu, desperately bored, and hungry for something to read. I found a book on my wife's bookshelf that I had somehow never seen before. It was called *This I Believe* with an even more intriguing subtitle—to me— of "Written for Edward R. Murrow." As an independent public radio producer for more than twenty years, I was curious to learn about something written for Murrow.

As it turns out, the book was a collection of essays based on a radio series of the same name hosted by the legendary broadcaster. To anyone who works in broadcasting, but especially in radio, Murrow is something like our patron saint.

I was surprised that I had never heard of this radio series before.

At first glance, I thought a fifty-year-old book filled with "the living philosophies of one hundred men and women in all walks of life" might be dry and dated. But I was wrong. It was as timely as could be. Not only was the content on these pages fascinating, but the idea behind the book—and radio series—captivated me as well: that all these writers had dug deeply inside themselves to discern what they truly believed—and then had the courage to share it with the world.

The original *This I Believe* radio series was the result of a lunch meeting in 1949 between Murrow, Philadelphia advertising executive Ward Wheelock, and CBS founder William S. Paley. The men bemoaned the spiritual state of the nation in the face of economic uncertainty, discrimination, the threat of nuclear war, and the rise of McCarthyism. To help counter this trend, they created this five-minute daily radio program in which the famous and the unknown would speak about the guiding beliefs by which they lived their lives.

The radio series launched in 1951 and quickly became a national phenomenon, airing on nearly 200 stations nationwide. More than ninety newspapers printed *This I Believe* pieces, usually as a weekly feature. Simon & Schuster published two best-selling compilations of essays, and Columbia Records released a popular two-album set of This I Believe statements as read by the authors.

In introducing the series, Murrow said, "We hardly need to be reminded that we are living in an age of confusion. A lot of us have traded in our beliefs for bitterness and cynicism, or for a heavy package of despair, or even a quivering portion of hysteria. Opinions can be picked up cheap in the marketplace, while such commodities as courage and fortitude and faith are in alarming short supply."

Those were the words that inspired me in 2003 to recreate This I Believe, nearly fifty years after Murrow's series ended. The country was deeply embroiled in the Iraq war to fight the terrorists "over there" so they wouldn't attack us "over here." One could easily substitute the terrorists of today for the Communist threat of the 1950s. And we were facing the Patriot Act, also eerily reminiscent of the McCarthy era.

Today, This I Believe, Inc., is a not-for-profit organization whose mission is engaging people in writing, sharing, and discussing the core values that guide our daily lives. By asking individuals from all walks of life to write and share 500-word essays on their personal philosophies, This I Believe encourages individuals to develop acceptance—and even respect—for beliefs different from one's own.

As I write this, in the fall of 2009, we have received more than 75,000 essays from across the nation and around the world. The popularity of the exercise stems from its simplicity: Write in the affirmative—say what you *do* believe, not what you *don't* believe. Speak in the first person, not the editorial "we." And limit the essay to 500 words so as to truly focus on the belief that is central to your life experience.

So, we in the twenty-first century follow in the giant footsteps of Edward R. Murrow to continue this mission of sharing and listening to one another so we may better understand one another. We consider ourselves stewards of this powerful idea, not only in showcasing the beliefs of a new generation, but in allowing people around the world to read the inspiring and still timely words of their parents' and grandparents' generation. Our hope is that the essays collected in this volume will speak to you across the decades—and help you consider your own beliefs of today.

Introduction to the 1950s
This I Believe *Radio Series*

Edward R. Murrow

THIS I BELIEVE. By that name, we bring you a new series of radio broadcasts presenting the personal philosophies of thoughtful men and women in all walks of life. In this brief time each night, a banker or a butcher, a painter or a social worker, people of all kinds who need have nothing more in common than integrity—a real honesty—will talk out loud about the rules they live by, the things they have found to be the basic values in their lives.

We hardly need to be reminded that we are living in an age of confusion. A lot of us have traded in our beliefs for bitterness and cynicism, or for a heavy package of despair, or even a quivering portion of hysteria. Opinions can be picked up cheap in the marketplace, while such commodities as courage and fortitude and faith are in alarmingly short supply. Around us all—now high like a distant thunderhead, now close upon us with the wet choking intimacy of a London fog—there is an enveloping cloud of fear.

There is a physical fear, the kind that drives some of us to flee our homes and burrow into the ground in the bottom of a Montana valley like prairie dogs to try to escape, if only for a little while, the sound and the fury of the A-bombs or the hell bombs or whatever may be coming. There is a mental fear which provokes others of us to see the images of witches in a neighbor's yard and stampedes us to burn down his house. And there is a creeping fear of doubt—doubt of what we have been taught, of the validity of so many things we have long since taken for granted to be durable and unchanging.

It has become more difficult than ever to distinguish black from white, good from evil, right from wrong. What truths can a human being afford to furnish the cluttered nervous room of his mind with when he has no real idea how long a lease he has on the future. It is to try to meet the challenge of such questions that we have prepared these broadcasts. It has been a difficult task and a delicate one. Except for those who think in terms of pious platitudes or dogma or narrow prejudice—and those thoughts we aren't interested in—people don't speak their beliefs easily or publicly.

In a way, our project has been an invasion of privacy, like demanding a man to let a stranger read his mail. General Lucius Clay remarked, "It would hardly be less embarrassing for an individual to be forced to disrobe in public than to unveil his private philosophy." Mrs. Roosevelt hesitated a long time. "What can I possibly say that will be of any value to anybody else," she asked us. And a railway executive in Philadelphia argued at first that we might as well try to engrave the Lord's Prayer on the head of a pin, as to attempt to discuss anything thoughtfully in the space of five minutes.

Yet, these people and many more have all made distinctive contributions of their beliefs to this series. You will hear from that inspiring woman, Helen Keller, who despite her blindness has lived a far richer life than most of us; from author Pearl Buck, sculptor William Zorach, businessmen and labor leaders, teachers and students. Perhaps we should warn you that there is one thing you won't hear, and that is a pat answer for the problems of life.

We don't pretend to make this time a spiritual or psychological patent medicine chest where one can come and get a pill of wisdom to be swallowed like an aspirin, to banish the headaches of our time. This reporter's beliefs are in a state of flux. It would be easier to enumerate the items I do not believe in, than the other way around. And yet, in talking to people, in listening to them, I have come to realize that I don't have a monopoly on the world's problems; others have their share, often far, far bigger than mine. This has helped me to see my own problems in truer perspective. And in learning how others have faced their problems, this has given me fresh ideas about how to tackle mine.

I hope as you listen to future programs on This I Believe, that they may be of assistance to you in a similar way.

EDWARD R. MURROW *hosted* This I Believe *from 1951 to 1955. The newsman gained acclaim for his CBS Radio broadcasts from London during World War II. His television documentaries for* See it Now *and* CBS Reports *tackled subjects ranging from Joseph McCarthy to farm-worker rights.*

The Secrets of Life

⁓

DR. AHMAD ZAKI ABU SHADI

AS A YOUNG MAN, I was greatly influenced by the stories I read about the heroism of great men of the past. What I learned of their love of freedom made a deep impression upon me. However, it was the merciless circumstances of my own experience which made book lessons secondary and led me to believe in and hold onto freedom as a hold onto life itself.

Gradually freedom became for me not only a synonym for life, but even for the Almighty. For the sake of freedom, I preferred to leave my country when tyranny was throwing independent thinkers into chains. In order to speak my mind and gain intellectual and spiritual liberty,

I suffered the material and moral hardships of voluntary exile. This, I found, was the inevitable price of the task I had set myself, that of upholding the principles of my beloved birthplace and serving the ideas in which I believe.

Life taught me all this, and I followed its teachings with confidence and ease, never regretting that I obeyed them. How could I regret what was simply justice to myself and my most deeply held principles? As much as I believed in freedom for myself, I believed in freedom for others and tried to realize it for them. Thus, I learned not to be egoistic, since egoism and loneliness are twins and both are contrary to human dignity. Likewise, I learned that endurance and perseverance are ingredients of this dignity. "The secret of life is but endurance, whether for the happy or the unhappy." However, it is endurance of the struggling fighter in the cause of a noble belief, which he preaches for the benefit of mankind, not the submission of the stricken coward that is a man.

Life taught me, as well, not to blame others as much as I blame myself for failures, which might have been avoided if I had been wiser and more wide awake. Hence, life taught me tolerance—even if I were slapped for it—for I found that toleration is an element of loftiness and loftiness is fundamental to human dignity. I always feel that the blow aimed at me does more real damage to the aggressor himself. Moreover, a tolerant attitude toward him makes him feel the meaning of this inevitable and automatic punishment, and often brings him back to the human fraternity. However, I have never believed in the toleration of evil at the expense of my dignity and idealism.

Finally, I leave it to time, the recorder; and to faith, the supervisor; to do justice to me and the principles in which I believe and for which I sacrifice. I know that justice will be done, though it may not come soon or ever be known. It is freedom which has made and sustained all that is worthwhile in me. It is a most precious treasure that life has granted me. To the extent that I have helped to preserve and enlarge it, I feel that I deserve life.

DR. AHMAD ZAKI ABU SHADI *was born in Cairo, studied medicine in London, and returned to Egypt to research bacteriology and teach. Also an accomplished artist, Abu Shadi published several collections of poetry, wrote scripts for operas, and painted. He immigrated to the United States in 1946.*

No Dream Is Impossible

~⌐

Julia Adams

From the time I can remember, I have wanted to be an actress. No one in my entire family had ever had artistic yearnings, so they looked upon my girlish dreams as a rather silly and impractical phase, which I would surely outgrow and then settle down in Arkansas like my more sensible cousins. But the dreams were still there when I reached the age of twenty, and I came to a rather shaky decision that I had to try it.

In the five years since that day, I've come to realize that whatever part of myself forced me to strike out rather haphazardly for Hollywood is the only real wisdom I possess. That part of me seemed to know that no matter how difficult achieving my goal might be, or even if I never achieved it, I would be happier striving toward my dream than if I tried to find security in a life I was unsuited for. This knowledge and quiet surety came from within me, and yet seemed to have its source far beyond comprehension of my wavering and indecisive personality. It alone kept me from quitting during that first year in which I discovered how right my family was in warning of the difficulties in store for me with no financial backing.

I found expensive dramatic lessons and living costs left almost nothing from my check as a secretary, with the very necessary clothes for studio interviews. But of course what really made me feel like catching the next bus for Arkansas was that in all the offices I managed to invade, not one casting man had looked at me with sudden interest and exclaimed, "That girl has something." My lovely air castles were quickly shattered, and I was forced to listen to the wiser, inner voice again. This time it had a new message: "Look at yourself honestly." Well this seemed simple enough, but it turned out to be very unpleasant indeed. One honest glance told me that only by unglamorous hard work over quite a few years would this gangling, unsure Arkansas girl be transformed into my dream of a fine actress.

After I recovered from the first shock of this discovery, to my surprise I began to feel stronger and more hopeful about the future. Since then I've found this inner voice always spoke the truth or made me try to find it for myself. Of course, I wandered away from it at times or rebelled when it said "no" to something I wanted very much at that moment. But these excursions away from my wiser self led only to confusion and unhappiness. Strangely enough, now that I've climbed a couple of rungs of the long ladder up, sometimes I find it harder to listen to the inner voice than when I was alone and struggling. It's a very quiet voice and is easily drowned out by outside babble. But one word from it is worth a book of advice from the best intentioned friends.

The voice seems very stern at times, as it makes me accept the responsibility for my failures and shortcomings, instead of excusing them or laying the blame elsewhere. But while it takes away petty egotism and silly pretensions, the voice whispers of things that send my thoughts and imagination soaring. It tells me no dream is impossible because faith in my inner self will guide me to its fulfillment. This belief in my inner self banishes fear and doubt and frees me to live and love and work to the fullest.

Television and film actress JULIA ADAMS' *career has spanned more than 50 years. In addition to her role in* Creature From the Black Lagoon, *Adams co-starred with movie icons John Wayne, Jimmy Stewart, Charlton Heston, and many others. More recently, she has appeared on television shows* Lost *and* Cold Case.

Does Anybody Believe an Actor?

———

Lionel Barrymore

First off, I think the world has come a mighty long way toward believing that what a man does to make a living can't rob him of his integrity as a human being, when it will listen to an actor talk about what he believes. I can remember when nobody believed an actor and didn't care what he believed. Why, the very fact that he was an actor made almost everything he said open to question, because acting was thought to be a vocation embraced exclusively by scatterbrains, show-offs, wastrels, and scamps. I don't believe that's true today and I don't think it ever was. I don't think there were ever any more ne'er-do-wells, rogues, poseurs, and villains in the acting profession than in any other line of work. At least I hope that's the case. If it isn't, it's too late to change my mind and much too late to change my profession.

The fact is, I think, every successful man today has prepared for his success by planning and living his life in much the same way that an actor plans and creates a part. We don't make anything up out of whole cloth when we decide the way we want to play a role, anymore than the author who wrote it made it up out of thin air. The author has one or two or perhaps a great many more models in mind from which he takes a little here and a little there until he's built up a new character out of substantial material. Now the actor who must play this part has to dig back into his life and recall one or two or more people who are, in some way, similar to the person the author put on paper. What I'm saying is, everybody connected with the actor's work had a model and copied this model, more or less exactly, adding to it here and there, until something new emerged.

I think this is the way a person must plan his life. Adopting, borrowing, and adapting a little here and a little there from his predecessors and his contemporaries, then adding a few touches until he's created himself.

I believe the difference between an eminently successful person and one whose life is just mediocre is the difference between a person who had an aim, a focus, a model upon which he superimposed his own life and one who didn't. To put it bluntly, you can't get anywhere unless you know where to start from and where to go.

The thing to be careful of in choosing a model is: don't aim too high for your capacity. It's necessary, it's true, to believe in the Almighty, but don't make Him your model. Have faith in Him but try for something you're more apt to make. Shoot a little closer to home. If you keep aiming at an attainable target, you can always raise your sights on another and more difficult one. But if you start off for the impossible, you're foredoomed to eternal failure.

I believe if a man remembers that, sets an attainable goal for himself, and works to attain it, conscious that when he does so he will then set another goal for himself, he will have a full, busy, and for this reason a happy life.

Stage, film, and radio actor LIONEL BARRYMORE *won an Academy Award for best actor for* A Free Soul *(1931). He appeared in more than 200 movies, including starring as Mr. Potter in* It's a Wonderful Life *and Disko in* Captains Courageous. *Barrymore was also an accomplished author, composer, artist, and director.*

Thought for Tomorrow

~⌐

Bernard Baruch

WHEN I WAS A YOUNGER MAN, I believed that progress was inevitable—that the world would be better tomorrow and better still the day after. The thunder of war, the stench of concentration camps, the mushroom cloud of the atomic bomb are, however, not conducive to optimism. All our tomorrows for years to come will be clouded by the threat of a terrible holocaust.

Yet my faith in the future, though somewhat shaken, is not destroyed. I still believe in it. If I sometimes doubt that man will achieve his mortal potentialities, I never doubt that he can.

I believe that these potentialities promise all men a measure beyond reckoning of the joys and comforts, material and spiritual, that life offers. Not Utopia, to be sure. I do not believe in Utopias. Man may achieve all but perfection.

Paradise is not for this world. All men cannot be masters, but none need to be a slave. We cannot cast out pain from the world, but needless suffering we can. Tragedy will be with us in some degree as long as there is life, but misery we can banish. Injustice will raise its head in the best of all possible worlds, but tyranny we can conquer. Evil will invade some men's hearts, intolerance will twist some men's minds, but decency is a far more common human attribute, and it can be made to prevail in our daily lives.

I believe all this because I believe, above all else, in reason—in the power of the human mind to cope with the problems of life. Any calamity visited upon man, either by his own hand or by a more omnipotent nature, could have been avoided or at least mitigated by a measure of thought. To nothing so much as the abandonment of reason does humanity owe its sorrows. Whatever failures I have known, whatever errors I have committed, whatever follies I have witnessed in private and public life, have been the consequence of action without thought.

Because I place my trust in reason, I place it in the individual. There is a madness in crowds from which even the wisest, caught up in their ranks, are not immune. Stupidity and cruelty are the attributes of the mob, not wisdom and compassion.

I have known, as who has not, personal disappointments

and despair. But always the thought of tomorrow has buoyed me up. I have looked to the future all my life. I still do. I still believe that with courage and intelligence we can make the future bright with fulfillment.

BERNARD BARUCH *rose to prominence as a financier and member of the New York Stock Exchange. He advised Presidents Woodrow Wilson during World War I, Franklin Roosevelt during the New Deal and World War II, and Harry Truman in the post-war era.*

Friendship Is a Passport

⸺⸺◯

JULIEN BRYAN

As a little boy, I believed devoutly in a very personal God who listened to my every word and took a very personal interest in all of my activities. I actually talked to Him a great deal. He was a God of love, but He was also a God of fierce and rapid justice. I felt as though His eyes were on me all the time.

I was raised a Protestant, and, as I look back, I can see that somewhere along the line I learned to be suspicious of and condescending to all other sects. Then, at seventeen, during the First World War, I joined the ambulance service of the French Army and served for six months at Verdun. My friends were simple French soldiers. With one or two exceptions, they were all Roman Catholics. I went to Mass with them, carried them when wounded, saw them die. And I came to like them as people, to admire their courage, to respect their right to their faith, which was so different from my own.

Twenty years ago, I began to make films about people all over the world. I took them as I found them—not as I wanted them to be. Wherever I went, I soon discovered that when you break bread with people and share their troubles and joys, the barriers of language, of politics, and of religion soon vanish. I liked them, and they liked me. That was all that mattered.

I came to find that the peoples of this world have much more in common with one another than they have differences. I have found this true wherever I have gone—even in Moscow and the far reaches of Siberia. The most hardened Communist would eventually break down if you were kind to his children. This was true even though he knew that he might be arrested the next day for becoming friendly with a foreigner.

As for the common man in Russia, my belief is that in spite of thirty-four years of Stalin and regimented thought-control, he still loves his land and his church and his family. And he hates the cruelty of the secret police and the incredible stupidity of the Soviet bureaucrats. In fact, I believe that in a fundamental way he is very much like us; he wants to live his own life—and be let alone.

All over the world I have watched the great religions in

practice: Buddhist monks at their devotions in Manchuria; Shinto priests in their temples in Japan; and only last autumn, the brave and hardy Serbian Muslims at their worship in Tito's Yugoslavia. I have come to hold a deep respect for all of man's great religions. And I have come to believe that despite their differences, all men can worship side by side.

For myself, I believe in people—and in their given right to enjoy the freedoms we so cherish in America. I believe in justice and knowledge and decent human values. I believe in each man's right to a job and food and shelter. And I sincerely believe that one day all of these things will come to pass.

My real faith, then, is a dream that in spite of daily headlines prophesying man's destruction, we can build a better world, a world of peace and human brotherhood. Yes, even in our lifetime! This is my faith and my dream. In my small way, I want to have a share in making it come about.

Documentary filmmaker JULIEN BRYAN *made educational movies exploring cultures as diverse as the nomadic tribes in Saudi Arabia and the mountain families of Appalachia. His films were translated into forty languages and shown around the world.*

Roll Away the Stone

———◡———

PEARL S. BUCK

I ENJOY LIFE because I am endlessly interested in people and their growth. My interest leads me to widen my knowledge of people, and this in turn compels me to believe in the common goodness of mankind. I believe that the normal human heart is born good. That is, it's born sensitive and feeling, eager to be approved and to approve, hungry for simple happiness and the chance to live. It neither wishes to be killed, not to kill. If through circumstances, it is overcome by evil, it never becomes entirely evil. There remain in it elements of good, however recessive, which continue to hold the possibility of restoration.

I believe in human beings, but my faith is without

sentimentality. I know that in environments of uncertainty, fear, and hunger, the human being is dwarfed and shaped without his being aware of it, just as the plant struggling under a stone does not know its own condition. Only when the stone is removed can it spring up freely into the light. But the power to spring up is inherent, and only death puts an end to it. I feel no need for any other faith than my faith in human beings.

Like Confucius of old, I am absorbed in the wonder of earth, and the life upon it, and I cannot think of heaven and the angels. I have enough for this life. If there is no other life, than this one has been enough to make it worth being born, myself a human being. With so profound a faith in the human heart and its power to grow toward the light, I find here reason and cause enough for hope and confidence in the future of mankind. The common sense of people will surely prove to them someday that mutual support and cooperation are only sensible for the security and happiness of all. Such faith keeps me continually ready and purposeful with energy to do what one person can towards shaping the environment in which the human being can grow with freedom. This environment, I believe, is based upon the necessity for security and friendship.

I take heart in a promising fact that the world contains food supplies sufficient for the entire earth population. Our knowledge of medical science is already sufficient to improve the health of the whole human race. Our resources and education, if administered on a world scale, can lift the intelligence of the race. All that remains is to discover how to administer upon a world scale the benefits which some of us already have. In other words, to return to my simile, the stone must be rolled away. This, too, can be done, as a sufficient number of human beings come to have faith in themselves and in each other. Not all will have such faith at the same moment, but there is a growing number who have the faith.

Half a century ago, no one had thought of world food, world health, world education. Many are thinking today of these things. In the midst of possible world war, of wholesale destruction, I find my only question this: Are there enough people now who believe? Is there time enough left for the wise to act? It is a contest between ignorance and death or wisdom and life. My faith in humanity stands firm.

PEARL S. BUCK *won the 1938 Nobel Prize in Literature for her writings including* The Good Earth. *Born in West Virginia to missionary parents, Buck lived in China for forty years. She wrote more than one hundred works and advocated for adoption of homeless Asian-American children.*

The Proud People of a Proud Country

James B. Carey

PERHAPS MORE THAN ANYTHING ELSE IN THE WORLD, I believe in liberty: liberty for myself, liberty for my fellow men. I cannot forget the legend engraved on the base of the Statue of Liberty on Bedlow's Island in New York Harbor: 'Give me your tired, your poor, your huddled masses yearning to breathe free, the wretched refuse of your teeming shore. Send these, the homeless tempest-tossed to me. I lift my lamp beside the golden door!' That is the voice of America.

As one small part of it, one tiny decibel in its sound, I, as a free individual of America, believe in it. It makes no boast of noble ancestry. On the contrary, it admits honestly that each of us in this country, with a possible and qualified exception of our native Indians, is a displaced person. In a particular kind of way, the Indian was our first displaced person. If you and I did not come from abroad ourselves, our forefathers did. The scores that drove them was economic, political, or religious oppression.

Oppression has always strewn the shores of life with wretched human refuse. We who today are the proud people of a proud country are what might be called the reclaimed refuse of other lands. The fact that the flotsam and the jetsam, the persecuted and the pursued of all these other lands, the fact that they came here and, for the most part, successfully started life anew, this renews my faith in the resilience of a human individual and the dignity of man.

There are those who say we should be content with the material benefits we have accrued among ourselves. I cannot accept that for myself. A laboring man needs bread and butter, and cash to pay the rent. But he would be a poor individual, indeed, if he were not able to furnish the vestibule of his mind and his soul with spiritual embellishments beyond the price of a union contract.

I mean by this that I believe it is important for a man to discover, whether he is an electrical worker or an executive, that he is an individual with his own resources and a sense of the dignity of his own person and that of other men. We are separate. We are collective. Man can be strong alone but not indomitable, in isolation. He has to belong to something, to realize he is not created separately or apart from the rest of mankind, whether he is an American or a Mohammedan. I am stirred by the abundance of the fields, the forest, the streams, and the natural resources they hold. But do these things make me important? Have we wrought the miracle of America because of these riches we hold? I say, no. Our strength—and I can say my strength, too, because I am a part of this whole—lies in a fundamental belief in the validity of human rights. And I believe that a man who holds these rights in proper esteem is greater, whether he is recognized or not.

As an individual, I must face the future with honesty and faith, in the good things that have made us mighty. I must have confidence in myself, in others, and all men of goodwill everywhere, for freedom is the child of truth and confidence.

Called "Labor's Boy Wonder," JAMES B. CAREY *was still in his twenties when he was elected national secretary of the Congress of Industrial Organizations. By age forty, Carey founded and became the first president of the International Union of Electrical, Radio, and Machine Workers.*

Guarding the Gift of Freedom

Lucius D. Clay

In the middle of the war against Hitler, if somebody had told me that I would one day be standing in the heart of Berlin before several hundred thousand of the citizens demonstrating their desire to be free, I would have said the person was crazy. Yet that very thing happened to me when I returned to the former German capital with the Freedom Bell, the symbol of the American campaign to pierce the Iron Curtain with the propaganda of truth. In open and dangerous defiance of the Russians and their East German puppets, thousands of West and East Berliners gathered in the middle of the city in a moving demonstration against tyranny. If they had believed in tyranny a few years before, they believed in it no longer. They had seen what democracy could mean and they wanted it.

I cite this incident to support my conviction that, given the proper circumstances, and some hope, man as an individual, wherever he may live, will demonstrate that he is inherently honest and decent. He wants little more than to live in friendship with his neighbor, in reasonable security, and to raise his children so they may find opportunity before them.

I think the troubled world in which we live should not dismay us. I believe the world today is historically a better world than the world of the past. Though ruthless men still maintain power through force and would extend power through conquest, people everywhere are becoming more tolerant and understanding than ever before. More peoples and more governments are willing to cooperate, to work together for peace and freedom, than at any time in history. At home we are more tolerant and understanding with each other, more willing to help our less fortunate neighbor here and abroad.

This, to me, is hopeful progress. It stems, I think, from the spread of freedom in which I believe and which I hold God gave us as a privilege. Like all precious possessions, freedom must be guarded carefully. I ask myself how I can best help guard it and the answer I find is citizenship. In my view, to be a good citizen does not require the holding of public office, the achievement of either political or financial success. But it does require that I vote from conviction, that I participate in community activities to the extent that I am able, that I be honest with myself and with others.

God has been good to us as a people. As I see it, we can return thanks for the position of leadership which we now hold in world affairs, only as we exercise this leadership to obtain freedom and peace. We can lead abroad only as we continue to improve our life at home, to become truly a land in which there is equal opportunity for all. This brings me back to the personal responsibility of the individual. I believe I can improve my life here and, perhaps, help others, only as I show pride in my country by finding the time to try to be a good citizen, and by being grateful to God for His goodness.

During World War II, General LUCIUS D. CLAY *was Director of Matériel for the Army and then Deputy Director for War Mobilization and Reconversion. After the war he was U.S. Military Governor of Germany. Clay ordered and organized the massive air-lift to feed people in Soviet-blockaded Berlin.*

The Human Equation

⟿

SUSAN PARKER COBBS

IT HAS NOT BEEN EASY for me to meet this assignment. We have so many changing and transitory beliefs besides the ones most central to our lives. I hope that what I say won't sound either too simple or too pious.

I know that it is my deep and fixed conviction that man has within him the force of good and a power to translate that force into life. For me, this means a pattern of life that makes personal relationships more important, a pattern that makes more beautiful and attractive the personal virtues: courage, humility, selflessness, and love.

I used to smile at my mother because the tears came so readily to her eyes when she heard or read of some incident that called out these virtues. I don't smile anymore, because I find I have become more and more responsive in the same inconvenient way to the same kind of story. And so, I believe, that I both can and must work to achieve the good that is in me. The words of Socrates keep coming back to me: "The unexamined life is not worth living." By examination, we can discover what is our good, and we can realize that knowledge of good means its achievement.

I know that such self-examination has never been easy. Plato maintained that it was "the soul's eternal search." It seems, to me, particularly difficult now. In a period of such rapid material expansion and such widespread conflicts, black and white have become gray and will not easily separate. There is a belief, which follows from this: If I have the potential of the good life within me and the compulsion to express it, then it is a power and a compulsion common to all men. What I must have for myself to conduct my search, all men must have: freedom of choice, faith in the power and the beneficent qualities of truth.

What frightens me most, today, is the denial of these rights because this can only come from the denial of, what seems to me, the essential nature of man. For if my conviction holds, man is more important than anything he's created, and our great task is to bring back again, into a subordinate position, the monstrous superstructures of our society.

I hope this way of reducing our problems to the human equation is not simply an evasion of them. I don't believe it is. For most of us, it is the only area in which we can work—the human area, with ourselves, with the people we touch—and through these, too, a vicarious understanding with mankind.

I watch young people these days wrestling with our mighty problems. They are much more concerned with them than my generation of students ever was. They are deeply aware of the words equality and justice. But in their great desire to right wrong, they are prone to forget that cult is a people—that nothing matters more than people. They need to add to their crusades the warmer and more affecting virtues of compassion and love. And here again come those personal virtues that bring tears to the eyes.

One further word: I believe that the power of good within us is real and comes there from a source outside and beyond ourselves. Otherwise, I could not put my trust so firmly in it.

SUSAN PARKER COBBS *was a teacher of Latin and Greek as well as Dean of Women at Swarthmore College. A native of Anniston, Alabama, Cobbs studied the classics at New York University and the University of Chicago. She taught at Swarthmore for nearly a quarter century.*

A Game of Cards

⁓

NORMAN COUSINS

EVER SINCE I WAS OLD ENOUGH TO READ BOOKS ON PHILOSOPHY, I have been intrigued by the discussions on the nature of man. The philosophers have been debating for years about whether man is primarily good or primarily evil, whether he is primarily altruistic or selfish, cooperative or combative, gregarious or self-centered, whether he enjoys free will or whether everything is predetermined.

As far back as the Socratic dialogues in Plato, and even before that, man has been baffled about himself. He knows he is capable of great and noble deeds, but then he is oppressed by the evidence of great wrongdoing.

And so he wonders. I don't presume to be able to resolve

the contradictions. In fact, I don't think we have to. It seems to me that the debate over good and evil in man, over free will and determinism, and over all the other contradictions—it seems to me that this debate is a futile one. For man is a creature of dualism. He is both good and evil, both altruistic and selfish. He enjoys free will to the extent that he can make decisions in life, but he can't change his chemistry or his relatives or his physical endowments—all of which were determined for him at birth. And rather than speculate over which side of him is dominant, he might do well to consider what the contradictions and circumstances are that tend to bring out the good or evil, that enable him to be a nobler and responsible member of the human race. And so far as free will and determinism are concerned, something I heard in India on a recent visit might be worth passing along. Free will and determinism, I was told, are like a game of cards. The hand that is dealt you represents determinism. The way you play your hand represents free will.

Now where does all this leave us? It seems to me that we ought to attempt to bring about and safeguard those conditions that tend to develop the best in man. We know, for example, that the existence of fear and man's inability to cope with fear bring about the worst in him. We know that what is true of man on a small scale can be true of society on a large scale. And today the conditions of fear in the world are, I'm afraid, affecting men everywhere. More than twenty-three hundred years ago, the Greek world, which had attained tremendous heights of creative intelligence and achievement, disintegrated under the pressure of fear. Today, too, if we read the signs correctly, there is fear everywhere. There is fear that the human race has exhausted its margin for error and that we are sliding into another great conflict that will cancel out thousands of years of human progress. And people are fearful because they don't want to lose the things that are more important than peace itself—moral, democratic, and spiritual values.

The problem confronting us today is far more serious than the destiny of any political system or even of any nation. The problem is the destiny of man: first, whether we can make this planet safe for man; second, whether we can make it fit for man. This I believe—that man today has all the resources to shatter his fears and go on to the greatest golden age in history, an age which will provide the conditions for human growth and for the development of the good that resides within man, whether in his individual or his collective being. And he has only to mobilize his rational intelligence and his conscience to put these resources to work.

NORMAN COUSINS *was editor of* The Saturday Review *for thirty-five years. A noted author, he detailed his fight against two life-threatening diseases in* Anatomy of an Illness *and* The Healing Heart. *In addition to his literary career, he was an ardent critic of the nuclear arms race and the Vietnam War.*

A Philosophy to Live By

⟶

JOHN CROMWELL

WHEN ASKED TO STATE MY BELIEF, it occurred to me that it was time to acquaint my older son with what I had discovered about the matter. And that perhaps if I wrote a letter to him about it, I might best answer this request. My older boy is fourteen.

Dear Jonathan,

When I was a young man just out of school starting to earn my living, my father began writing letters to me full of good counsel and the wisdom of his experience. His letters were written out of love and great anxiety, the desire to acquaint me with certain truths and thereby spare me some—perhaps just one or two—of the mistakes he had made and now saw so clearly.

Any true philosophy, I'm sure, evolves from so many varied experiences. It is made up of such an infinite variety of things heard and seen and felt, that you might spend years thinking about it before you found the proper words to help others understand it. For me, there are several things I believe, deeply, for they evolved slowly out of my experience without my being aware of it.

We do a great deal of talking to ourselves, haven't you noticed? Somewhere along the line, it occurred to me it might be worthwhile to get to know this other fellow I was forever talking to. I might, for one thing, begin to get along with him better. And then, he always seemed to know more about me than I did about him, and that struck me as a great disadvantage to me. So I decided to become better acquainted with this other fellow. And so, I began to know more about myself.

One of the first things I discovered was that I did not like to be fooled. I had had that experience when that other fellow had fooled me, and it caused me no end of embarrassment. And, too, I saw other men who were being fooled and didn't even catch on, and I realized how much harm it did them and the world they were trying to live in.

I saw that one of the first things I must insist on in this

new acquaintanceship was complete and relentless honestly. That was the only way I could ever know where I stood with this other fellow. And of almost greater importance, it was the only way I could ever know where I stood with other men, with the world I was to live and work in. Every man is liable to find himself, at some time, in a situation where everyone else disagrees with him. That is when he must know that fellow he talks things over with—has to know there is no compromise in him—so that when this fellow tells him he is right, it hardly matters what anyone else says.

After I believed in this step in the relationship, it didn't take me long to see that I might have a very hard time deceiving anyone. Not that I wanted to, of course, quite the contrary. But the stresses of living are sometimes rapid and sometimes heavy, and very often insinuating and plausible. Your mind can take countless turnings to satisfy desires and appetites. At that point, because he knows you so well, this other fellow won't let you respond to anything but the truth—stark and unadorned.

Now in closing, Jonathan, let me say that the discovery of a philosophy to live by is a healing thing. It brings its discoverer about as close to achieving happiness as it is possible to get. This won't mean much to you for a long time. That it someday may is the fervent hope of your affectionate father.

JOHN CROMWELL *directed more than fifty films, including* Of Human Bondage, The Prisoner of Zenda, *and* Dead Reckoning. *As an actor, Cromwell won the 1952 Tony Award for Best Actor for his performance in* Point of No Return. *He is the father of actor James Cromwell.*

An Honest Doubter

~

Elizabeth Deutsch

At the age of sixteen, many of my friends have already chosen a religion to follow (usually that of their parents), and are bound to it by many ties. I am still "free-lancing" in religion, searching for beliefs to guide me when I am an adult. I fear I shall always be searching, never attaining ultimate satisfaction, for I possess that blessing and curse—a doubting, questioning mind.

At present, my doubting spirit has found comfort in certain ideas, gleaned from books and experience, to form a personal philosophy. I find that this philosophy—a code consisting of a few phrases—supplements, but does not replace, religion.

The one rule that could serve anyone in almost any situation is, "To see what must be done and not to do it, is a crime." Urged on by this, I volunteer for distasteful tasks or pick up scrap paper from the floor. I am no longer able to ignore duty without feeling guilty. This is "the still, small voice," to be sure, but sharpened by my own discernment of duty.

"The difficult we do at once, the impossible takes a little longer." This is the motto of a potential scientist, already struggling to unravel the mysteries of life. It rings with the optimism youth needs in order to stand up against trouble or failure.

Jonathan Edwards, a Puritan minister, resolved never to do anything out of revenge. I am a modern, a member of a church far removed from Puritanism, yet I have accepted this resolution. Since revenge and retaliation seem to have been accepted by nations today, I sometimes have difficulty reconciling my moral convictions with the tangled world being handed down to us by the adults. Apparently what I must do to make life more endurable, is to follow my principles, with the hope that enough of this feeling will rub off on my associates to begin a chain reaction.

To a thinking person, such resolutions are very valuable; nevertheless, they often leave a vacuum in the soul. Churches are trying to fill this vacuum, each by its own method. During this year, I have visited churches ranging from orthodoxy to extreme liberalism. In my search for a personal faith, I consider it my duty to expose myself to all forms of religion. Each church has left something within me—either a new concept of God and man, or an understanding and respect for those of other beliefs. I have found such experiences with other religions the best means for freeing myself from prejudices.

Through my visits, the reasoning of fundamentalists has become clearer to me, but I am still unable to accept it. I have a simple faith in the Deity and a hope that my attempts to live a decent life are pleasing to Him. If I were to discover that there is no afterlife, my motive for moral living would not be destroyed. I have enough of the philosopher in me to love righteousness for its own sake.

This is my youthful philosophy, a simple, liberal, and optimistic feeling, though I fear I shall lose some of it as I become more adult. Already, the thought that the traditional thinkers might be right, after all, and I wrong, has made me waver. Still, these are my beliefs at sixteen. If I am mistaken, I am too young to realize my error. Sometimes, in a moment of mental despair, I think of the words, "God loves an honest doubter," and am comforted.

When ELIZABETH DEUTSCH *was sixteen, she won a* This I Believe *essay contest in the* Cleveland Press *newspaper. Her prize was a trip to New York City to record her essay for broadcast on the original series. Deutsch went on to become a professor of plant breeding at Cornell University.*

What Makes Me Feel Big

J. FRANK DOBIE

"MY MIND IS BIG WHEN I LOOK AT YOU AND TALK TO YOU," Chief Eagle of the Pawnees said to George Bird Grinnell when, after years of absence, that noble writer appeared at his friend's tepee.

It is very difficult in drawing up a credo to be severely honest about one's self, to avoid all traditional cant. We actually believe in what we value most. Outside of the realms of carnality and property, which men appearing in public generally pretend not to notice, I believe in and draw nourishment from whatever makes me feel big.

I believe in a Supreme Power, unknowable and impersonal, whose handiwork the soul-enlarging firmament declares. However, I believe in questionings, doubtings, searchings, skepticism, and I discredit credulity or blind faith. The progress of man is based on disbelief of the commonly accepted. The noblest minds and natures of human history have thought and sung, lived and died, trying to budge the status quo towards a larger and fuller status.

I am sustained by a belief in evolution—the increasing purpose of life in which the rational is, with geological slowness, evolving out of the irrational. To believe that goodness and wisdom and righteousness, in Garden of Eden perfection, lie somewhere far ahead instead of farther and farther behind, gives me hope and somewhat explains existence. This is a long view. I do not pretend that it is a view always present in me. It does raise me when I have it, however.

I feel no resentment so strongly as that against forces which make men and women afraid to speak out forthrightly. The noblest satisfaction I have is in witnessing the up movement of suppressed individuals and people. I make no pretense to having rid myself of all prejudices, but at times when I have discovered myself freed from certain prejudices, I have felt rare exhilaration.

For me, the beautiful resides in the physical, but it is spiritual. I have never heard a sermon as spiritual in either phrase or fact as, "Waters on a starry night are beautiful and free." No hymn lifts my heart higher than the morning call of the bobwhite or the long fluting cry of sandhill cranes out of the sky at dusk. I have never smelled incense in a church as refining to the spirit as a spring breeze laden with aroma from a field of bluebonnets.

Not all hard truths are beautiful, but beauty is truth. It incorporates love and is incorporated by love. It is the goal of all great art. Its presence everywhere makes it free to'all. It is not so abstract as justice, but beauty and intellectual freedom and justice, all incorporating truth and goodness, are constant sustainers to my mind and spirit.

Educator and folklorist J. FRANK DOBIE *wrote numerous books and articles about vanishing ways of life on the ranches of his native Texas. He taught in the English department at the University of Texas for many years and was a lecturer on U.S. history at Cambridge during World War II.*

I Don't Play to the Grandstand

BOBBY DOERR

IT SEEMS TO ME THAT WHAT ANY MAN'S BELIEFS ARE depends upon how he spends his life. I've spent a good part of mine as a professional baseball player and the game that I play for a living is naturally a very important thing to me. I've learned a lot of things on the baseball diamond about living—things that have made me happier and, I hope, a better person.

I've found that when I make a good play and take my pitcher off the hook, it's just natural for me to feel better than if I made a flashy play that doesn't do anything except make me look good for the grandstands. It works the same way off the ball field, too. Doing a good turn for a neighbor, a friend, or even a stranger gives me much more satisfaction than doing something that helps only myself. It's as if all people were my teammates in this world and things that make me closer to them are good, and things that make me draw away from them are bad.

Another belief very important to me is that I am only as good as my actual performance proves that I am. If I cannot deliver, then my name and reputation don't mean a thing. I thought of this when in the season of 1951 I told my team that I would not play in 1952. I reached this decision because I realized that I wouldn't be able to give my best performance to the people who would pay my salary by coming through the turnstiles. I don't see how anyone can feel right about success or fame that is unearned. For me, most of the satisfaction in any praise I receive comes from the feeling that it is the reward for a real effort I have made.

Many ball players talk a lot about luck and figure that it is responsible for their successes and failures, on and off the field. Some of them even carry around a rabbit's foot and other good-luck charms, or they have superstitions they go through to make sure of things going the way they want them to. I've never been able to go along with people who believe that way. I've got a feeling that there's something deeper and more important behind the things that happen to me and whether they turn out good or bad. It seems to me that many of the things which some people credit to luck are the results of Divine assistance. I can't imagine an all-wise, all-powerful God that isn't interested in the things I do in my life. Believing this makes me always want to act in such a way as to deserve the things that the Lord will do for me.

Maybe that's the most important thing of all. Doing good in order to deserve good. A lot of wonderful things have happened to me in my lifetime. I've had a long, rewarding career in organized baseball. The fans have been swell to me, and I've always liked my teammates. But what really matters is that I've got just about the best folks that anyone could ask for. Doing what I can to make things more pleasant for my father and mother, and for my wife and our son, has been one of the things I have enjoyed most because it seems to be a way for me to pay back something of what I owe them for all the encouragement and pleasure they've given me.

I guess the best way to sum it all up is that I'm happy to be around and I'd like to be able to make other people glad of it, too.

BOBBY DOERR *was second baseman for the Boston Red Sox from 1937 to 1951. He played in nine All-Star Games and was elected to the Baseball Hall of Fame in 1986. Doerr retired to the land in rural Oregon he bought when he was a teenager.*

My Father's Evening Star

WILLIAM O. DOUGLAS

DURING MOMENTS OF SADNESS OR FRUSTRATION, I often think of a family scene years ago in the town of Yakima, Washington. I was about seven or eight years old at the time. Father had died a few years earlier. Mother was sitting in the living room talking to me, telling me what a wonderful man Father was. She told me of his last illness and death. She told me of his departure from Cleveland, Washington, to Portland, Oregon...for what proved to be a fatal operation. His last words to her were these: "If I die it will be glory, if I live it will be grace." I remember how those words puzzled me. I could not understand why it would be glory to die. It would be glory to live, that I could understand. But why it would be glory to die was something I did not understand until later.

Then one day in a moment of great crisis I came to understand the words of my father. "If I die it will be glory, if I live it will be grace." That was his evening star. The faith in a power greater than man. That was the faith of our fathers. A belief in a God who controlled man in the universe, that manifested itself in different ways to different people. It was written by scholars and learned men in dozens of different creeds. But riding high above all secular controversies was a faith in One who was the Creator, the Giver of Life, the Omnipotent.

Man's age-long effort has been to be free. Throughout time he has struggled against some form of tyranny that would enslave his mind or his body. So far in this century, three epidemics of it have been let loose in the world.

We can keep our freedom through the increasing crisis of history only if we are self-reliant enough to be free—dollars, guns, and all the wondrous products of science and the machine will not be enough. "This night thy soul shall be required of thee."

These days I see graft and corruption reach high into government. These days I see people afraid to speak their minds because someone will think they are unorthodox and therefore disloyal. These days I see America identified more and more with material things, less and less with spiritual standards. These days I see America drifting from the Christian faith, acting abroad as an arrogant, selfish, greedy nation, interested only in guns and dollars, not in people and their hopes and aspirations.

These days the words of my father come back to me more and more. We need his faith, the faith of our fathers. We need a faith that dedicates us to something bigger and more important than ourselves or our possessions. Only if we have that faith will we be able to guide the destiny of nations, in this the most critical period of world history.

WILLIAM O. DOUGLAS *was an associate justice of the U.S. Supreme Court from 1939 to 1975. As a boy, he hiked the Cascade Mountains near his home in Washington to strengthen legs weakened by polio. His prolific career on the bench was marked by controversy and two attempts to impeach him.*

We Do Not Live Alone

John Davis Drummey

To sum up my credo in a sentence: The farther away I get from myself, the nearer I get to God.

Most of my troubles came when I was obsessed with my own petty concerns and trivial details. I respect the hermit but admire the crusader—his life takes more courage. I sympathize with the introvert as I would with the sickly, but both are missing a lot of life.

As a Catholic, I am touched by Assisi and his animals, but Loyola and his army fascinate me. No man ever got as much out of life as G. K. Chesterton, and he remarked, "Here dies another day during which I have had eyes, ears, hands, and the great world around me. And with tomorrow begins another. Why am I allowed two?"

Today's young people live years in what used to be days. I might be a good example. I've been married six years, have two children, a home, and have been recently honored by my college, the Jewish community, and the Chamber of Commerce. I direct the region of a famous human-relations agency. I've had much sickness, been in a war, worked at a newspaper, traveled all over America and half the world, graduated from college, ran my own ad business, worked three years as an executive for General Electric, lost two brothers in a family, and spent a year in a tuberculosis sanatorium.

Now I could go on in this personal basis, but the point is I've just reached the thirty mark. Many of these experiences would be denied in the past age. I've found that the beliefs I've discovered in the twenty- to thirty-year period can be the ground floor of my philosophy, and that these early years can be a fruitful basis for a mature life for everyone. I remember in particular two young men named Jefferson and Hamilton, whose thoughts are deeply embedded in this country's philosophy.

I like people because they are the key to the great human values: love, charity, friendship, sacrifice, and brotherhood. Some of my closest friends are people whom I was at first hesitant to meet. What close calls. I feel sorry for those poor souls who must go through life not knowing their neighbors, not participating in groups or being active in causes, and when I meet persons who are not interested in people who are different—and of course, that's everyone. Then I re-dedicate myself to this thing called society—a continuous living drama equal to anything Hollywood ever produced. I believe the more people you understand, the more you understand God.

I have had in my short life a multitude of illnesses, close calls, disappointments, sufferings, and personal crosses. But I honestly think I could have survived them better, and per-haps avoided some of them altogether, if I'd gotten away from an obsession with myself. This philosophy is not star-tling for its originality nor for its maturity. It is not the whole faith I have, for in this short space I omitted the necessities of religion, introspection, study, family, and the other funda-mentals which are done without the crowd.

But my main point is that we do not live alone in this contracting globe unless the belief in belonging to the hu-man race is most important now, with bomb tensions, rabid nationalism, and rampant suspicion. And when I see a hard-bitten lawyer happily planning an outing for blind children; when I watch men of great prestige and wealth put their efforts into brotherhood; when I observe men and women begin to grow out of their own little tiny shells by going into the world and maturing by knowing other peoples, other greater sorrows, other new shared joys; then I know that this is worth believing in.

JOHN DAVIS "JACK" DRUMMEY *had a long career in advertising and public relations despite being a disabled veteran of World War II. He was also a cartoonist for several publications and wrote "The Observant Bostonian" column for* Boston *magazine for many years.*

The Job of Citizenship

⌐

GENEVIEVE EARLE

MY EARLY AND UNFORGETTABLE EXPERIENCE OF CITY LIFE occurred more than fifty years ago when, as a young country-bred girl, I rode with my mother on the Third Avenue elevated in New York City. As the train clattered along that dirty thoroughfare, I gazed into the interiors of those dark, untidy, and crowded flats with a profound sense of shock. I asked my mother why people had to live that way. She explained that they were poor and could afford no better homes.

I do not recall that I made any conscious pledge to find out why such things had to be, but many years later when I studied the social sciences and economics, the remembrance of this preventable squalor returned with a renewed awareness. Still later, having undertaken private social and community work as a career, I began to realize that splendid and essential as these efforts may have been, I was trying to bail out an ocean of misery with a teacup. I became convinced that the city itself was our greatest social worker because it was spending greater sums for related or similar work than all the private welfare agencies combined. I saw city government as a focal point of an ever-increasing program of service, a partnership which its citizens shared equally, designed to promote those things that are good and to combat those things that are evil.

Archimedes explained the principle of fulcrum by saying, "Show me the place to stand and I can move the world." To me, this place is city government; touch that and you touch the whole community. Thus the weight of a finger at the right place can set in motion forces that can create a wholesome, decent environment for all people and mold our way of living a little nearer to our heart's desire.

The fight for good government, while a winning one, is never permanently won. It must be waged afresh each day. To keep eternally at this job is an act of faith and courage. To those who are fainthearted or faltering, may I end by quoting from the oath of the young men of Athens. "We will never bring disgrace to this, our city, by any act of dishonesty or cowardice. We will fight for our ideals and sacred things of the city, both alone and with many. We will revere and obey the city's laws and do our best to incite a like respect in those above us who are prone to annul, and set them at naught. We will strive unceasingly to quicken the public sense of civic duty. Thus in all these ways we will transmit this city, not only not less, but far greater and more beautiful than it was transmitted to us."

The job of being an alert, active citizen is exciting, relatively easy, and wholly rewarding. My many years of civic work—as a citizen and as a public official—convinced me that if each one of us did his or her share and lived up to the spirit of this oath, that his town, his nation, and the world would be a happier and a very better place to live in. In this I believe.

GENEVIEVE B. EARLE *was a social worker and head of the Brooklyn branch of the League of Women Voters. In 1937, she became the first woman to be elected to the New York City Counsel, where she served as minority leader of the body.*

Cooperation Works Better than Conflict

~~~~~~~~~~~~~~~

ALEXANDER FORBES

THE NOTION THAT SCIENCE AND RELIGION are antagonistic and incompatible seems, to me, utterly false. Science is the quest for eternal truths in the universe by disciplined minds, and I am sure that if pursued in the right spirit, science engenders reverence. Reverence and worship are as much part of the normal human being as hunger for food, or zest for action. Primitive man, naturally, worships the sun—prime source of light and warmth, and indeed of this earth, itself. I sympathize and find the blue sky overhead as noble a setting for worship as the temple or cathedral.

I disagree with the cynics, who hold that all organized religion is a racket conducted by parasites who fleece the gullible. The history of religions reveals examples of just that. Indeed, our present civilization is not fully free from that reproach. But I am sure the well nigh universal tendency of man to revere, and worship, and to build his noblest edifices for the purpose, means more than wholesale surrender to self-seeking parasites. Religion is not a weakness. It is a vital element in human nature.

Geology tells the story of the change in our planet through millions of years from a mass of molten matter, in which no life could exist, to a fit abode for living creatures. Biology takes up the story and tells how life has evolved from origins as primitive as the protean molecule, to ever more highly organized forms—animals that see, hear, and feel, much as we do—and through them to human beings, who can reason, cultivate the fine arts, and organize a cooperative and harmonious society.

I find in this cosmic sequence a profoundly stirring drama. Those who say that all this is just a complex of physical and chemical reactions, devoid of meaning or purpose, are blinding themselves to all that matters most in our lives. If a chemist analyzes a volume of Shakespeare and finds nothing there but paper and ink, his report is quite irrelevant to me as I read Hamlet. Analysis of a symphony by physical apparatus may appear complete to the physicist, but it means nothing to the musician.

Viewing the pageant of the universe in its entirety and contemplating man's rise from the protozoan to his highest spiritual stature, I find in the creative force that did all this, something we can worship with all the reverence that is in us. In the struggle for survival through the ages, cruel competition has been stressed as a necessary element. Yet, in spite of this, many animals lower in the scale than man have found that cooperation works better than conflict, and actually promotes survival. How much more does this apply to civilized man?

I believe that when neighbor countries learn that friendly trade is better than warfare, they will live better. When management and labor learn that their common aim— production—is better served by teamwork than by quarrels and strikes, they will fare better physically and spiritually.

I deplore the hostile conflicts between rival churches calling themselves Christian. The need for worship is expressed in many ways. The creeds and rituals that suit one type of mind do not satisfy others. Dogmatic insistence that one form of worship is right and all others wrong is as alien to the spirit of freedom, to which our Western world is dedicated, as the tyranny of the dictator. Only when mutual respect and friendly cooperation replace dogmatism and bigotry will the true spirit of liberty prevail on earth.

DR. ALEXANDER FORBES *was a pioneer in the field of neurophy-siology. He graduated from Harvard Medical School in 1910 and devoted himself to research on the human nervous system. Forbes served as a professor emeritus of physiology at Harvard for many years.*

An Athlete of God

~——

MARTHA GRAHAM

I BELIEVE THAT WE LEARN BY PRACTICE. Whether it means to learn to dance by practicing dancing, or to learn to live by practicing living, the principles are the same. In each, it is the performance of a dedicated, precise set of acts, physical or intellectual, from which come shape of achievement, the sense of one's being, the satisfaction of spirit. One becomes in some area an athlete of God. Practice means to perform over and over again, in the face of all obstacles, some act of vision, of faith, of desire. Practice is a means of inviting the perfection desired.

I think the reason dance has held such an ageless magic for the world is that it has been the symbol of the performance of living. Many times, I hear the phrase, "the dance of life." It is close to me for a very simple and understandable reason. The instrument through which the dance speaks is also the instrument through which life is lived: the human body. It is the instrument by which all the primaries of experience are made manifest. It holds in its memory all matters of life and death and love.

Dancing appears glamorous, easy, delightful. But the path to the paradise of that achievement is not easier than any other. There is fatigue so great that the body cries even in its sleep. There are times of complete frustration. There are daily small deaths. Then, I need all the comfort that practice has stored in my memory and the tenacity of faith. But it must be the kind of faith that Abraham had, wherein he "staggered not at the promise of God through unbelief."

It takes about ten years to make a mature dancer. The training is twofold. There is the study and practice of the craft in order to strengthen the muscular structure of the body. The body is shaped, disciplined, honored, and in time, trusted. The movement becomes clean, precise, eloquent, truthful. Movement never lies. It is a barometer telling the state of the soul's weather to all who can read it. This might be called the law of the dancer's life, the law which governs its outer aspects.

Then, there is the cultivation of the being. It is through this that the legends of the soul's journey are retold with all their gaiety and their tragedy and the bitterness and sweetness of living. It is at this point that the sweep of life catches up the mere personality of the performer, and while the individual—the undivided one—becomes greater, the personal becomes less personal. And there is grace. I mean the grace resulting from faith...faith in life, in love, in people, in the act of dancing. All this is necessary to any performance in life which is magnetic, powerful, rich in meaning.

In a dancer there is a reverence for such forgotten things as the miracle of the small beautiful bones and their delicate strength. In a thinker there is a reverence for the beauty of the alert and directed and lucid mind. In all of us who perform, there is an awareness of the smile, which is part of the equipment, or gift, of the acrobat. We have all walked the high wire of circumstance at times. We recognize the gravity of pull on the Earth as he does. The smile is there because he is practicing living at that instant of danger. He does not choose to fall.

In seven decades as a dancer and choreographer, MARTHA GRAHAM created 181 ballets. A founder of modern dance, she is known for her collaborations with other leading artists, including composer Aaron Copland. Graham's company trained dance greats such as Alvin Ailey and Twyla Tharp.

A Rationalist Within Reason

Albert Guerard

I was born in Paris within a stone's throw of the Louvre. For nearly a decade in my formative years, London became the second home of my spirit. I felt to the full the charm of the vast chaotic metropolis, even the fog which wrapped that great center of power and trade in dream and mystery.

My father was a free-thinking Catholic—not an unusual combination in the land of Montaigne and Voltaire. My mother belonged to the pitiful remnant of the Gallican church. My wife's family were of Scottish-Courlando descent. From these conflicting experiences, I have retained an odd blend of ideals, a deep love for long-rooted things, meadow books, old cities, ancient creeds. And also the sense that these were but toys and garments for the eternal and ever new thoughts of living man. The Tory and the radical within me smile indulgently and fraternally at each other.

The Dreyfus case taught me that the noblest tradition, when exclusive and infallible in its own conceit, could become a power of evil. I was bidden to the nation, the army, the flag, but these were laid against justice, and justice had to prevail. "My country right or wrong," is the most insidious of blasphemies. It means thou shalt have no other God beside their country, not even God.

I found myself at home from the very first in the America of 1906, an America deeply attached to its brief past but first of all to its principles, which were shaping the future. An America which was admirably defined by David Star Jordan as "the land where hate dies away." The America I had found in 1906 had erected a statue to William Lloyd Garrison with the inscription, "My country is the world. My countrymen are all mankind."

I have remained an obstinate liberal in the strictest sense of the term—a lover of liberty—throughout the half-century of my American life. I have steadfastly combated the dogmatic exclusive systems which seek to crush man's free spirit with their leaden feet. Partisanship and sectarianism I regard as wholly evil. They breed fanaticism in its blind, self-righteous cruelty.

I call myself a rationalist within reason. And I strive to be a do-gooder with a critical spirit. Those who sneer at a desire to do right, those who believe that evil, force, pride, greed is a safer guide than good, those men may call themselves realists and win pitiful little victories, but in truth they are the militant atheists. They are hampering the slow ascent of mankind out of the primeval slime into a freer, gentler, more humane world.

The key to the good is love or, in Christian terms, charity. My creed against the materialist, the realist, and the doctrinaires may be summed up in these words: "Faith is the hope that charity is not vain."

ALBERT GUERARD *came to America in 1906 and served as an Army intelligence officer in World War I. He later taught French and comparative literature at more than a dozen colleges and universities, including Stanford and UCLA, and he wrote twenty-eight books.*

The Power of Self-Preservation

HUGO HAAS

THERE ARE MANY THINGS I LEARNED TO BELIEVE IN during the many years of my eventful life. First of all, I learned to believe in the tremendous power of life itself and in the power of self-preservation. Through the stormy years of persecution, exile, poverty, and grief over the losses of people nearest to me, I never lost the drive to go on, even in situations of hopelessness and despair. The power of self-preservation teaches you to believe in many good things—for instance, in the fundamental goodness of people.

Throughout the bad years of misfortune, there always appeared from nowhere, somebody—people, simple people, who were willing to help. Sometimes it almost seemed incredible that complete strangers would be interested in my existence. I finally arrived at the conclusion that it is not so easy to die of hunger and starvation, that there is always someone, somewhere, hidden behind your door and waiting with a piece of bread to spoil your honest intention to die and insisting in your continuing to live.

I believe in the might of nature, and I can never get tired of daily little miracles like sunrises and sunsets, flowers and trees, the firmament and elements around us. I believe strongly in the joy of creation, in useful work, in expressing and exchanging views, philosophies, and feeling.

I believe in beauty such as music, paintings, books, sculptures, expressions of emotions in all fields of art. I also believe in simplicity and logic. I don't believe in art that has to be explained to me. Art must talk plainly for itself and to anybody equally. In the length of years, in the progress of time, one can learn to adjust oneself to understand new harmonies in music and new lights and colors in paintings, new and more daring ideas in books. But basically, one should never abandon the principles of simplicity and logic.

I believe in friendship as something given by God to make our lives worthwhile, warm, and less lonesome. And I believe in love with all the consequences of joy, sorrow, and sacrifices. For love is the strongest element that in the final analysis fulfills our lives. It is the strongest impression left to the end of our days and all the dear faces connected to these feelings—father and mother, brothers and sisters, wife and children—stay with us in our memories to the very last moments of our consciousness.

I believe also in the comfort of a clear conscience, which makes me feel safe in looking into my neighbor's eyes. I believe in freedom, and I believe in democracy. I have lived now in America for thirteen years, and the feeling of freedom and security and justice became to me more important than all the material advantages, and I'm deeply grateful.

Summing up all my beliefs, which I gathered during the years of my rich life and experience, I believe strongly in some great unknown power, which guides our life and is responsible for everything that is worthwhile to enjoy and to endure, may he be called Christ, Jehovah, Confucius, or Mohammed.

Film actor, writer, director, and producer HUGO HAAS *was born in Brno, Moravia (now the Czech Republic). His father and brother died in Nazi gas chambers, but Hugo escaped to America. He became active in Hollywood making numerous low-budget movies. Haas died in 1968.*

Love and the Unceasing Wonder of Life

—◦

MR. AND MRS. OLIVER HALE

MRS. HALE: On sudden impulse the other day, my husband sat down and, in a few minutes, wrote out the beliefs which follow. They are my beliefs, too, since they evolved from our lives together. Our lives have been so closely intertwined that he speaks of them as if they were a single unit.

MR. HALE: As two people united in a good marriage for thirty years, we have come to a time when we must face the time of separation. Normally, this aroused in both a fear of being left alone and dread of a future in which the other is absent. The prospect would seem to be bleak, but remarkably, it is not so. The world, possessed by the survivor, would still be a place of lively and insistent interest. It would still be breathtakingly beautiful. The heavens would continuously proclaim to the imagination the unfathomable and the infinite.

Love runs through our united life like a stream, and because it has been a great irrigating force, the days are always green. We have had little barrenness, whether of the mind or the spirit. Because we have loved each other as unselfishly as is humanly possible, we find it natural to love our fellow man. We are not saints. Human behavior is sometimes unforgivable. We do not condone the great crimes against peoples or the little crimes individually perpetrated. It is difficult to pardon them. It is difficult not to ask revenge or punishment. But there was one who had compassion in His heart for the multitude and for the sinner. We do not presume to measure our very human attitude against the blinding divinity of that great spirit, but love calls out in our hearts for compassion, for understanding.

We believe in man's innate goodness, as much as we believe in a child's natural innocence. We believe that the achievements of man are greater than his failures. We believe in man's essential goodness, in his soul's aspiration, whether toward his god or in search of an answer to his being. At night, or at other quiet times, reading the great books, listening to the great music, we are moved to believe that all being is longing after something—a cry from the deepest recesses of the heart. But it does not seem to answer, except that we believe, and many do not, and they are most lost. Shall we not, then, have compassion upon them?

We believe in this—we, two people, united in a long marriage that has been marked by love and understanding. We have neither fame nor wealth and are known to a very small number of people. We are obscure and of the great majority. But we have known love and found it good, and we have tried to live compassionately and to be just to our fellow man. And when someday we shall separate, as we indeed must, the one who remains will grieve and be sad, but the power of love will act as a strong and continuing will to live and to marvel at the unceasing wonder of life and the universe.

OSCAR AND ESTHER HIRSCHMANN *lived in New York City, where Oscar was a poet writing under the pen name of Oliver Hale. Their essay was the only statement in the original* This I Believe *series to be delivered by two people.*

Freedom Is a Social Necessity

ARTHUR GARFIELD HAYS

THIS I BELIEVE: that progress comes from struggle, conflict, and competition of ideas; that freedom is an end in itself—almost as important to the individual as the food he eats or the air he breathes. I believe that the best expression of freedom is in our Bills of Rights, and that not only our welfare but our safety as a nation depends upon our observance of the principles expressed in the Bills of Rights.

Freedom is a social luxury, say some. History proves that freedom is a social necessity. All this is regarded as platitudinous by most Americans. Yet, there are differences in interpretation. Take freedom of speech, for example. Most people believe not in freedom of speech; they believe in "freedom of speech, but." I believe in the right of anyone to express any opinion, no matter how wild, radical, blasphemous, or loathsome such opinion might be, and no matter how unpopular, vicious, or discredited the speaker may be.

Mark you, I'm not talking of incitements to violence or violations of law; those are not opinions. Thought must be free. Men cannot think unless they express themselves. Is this an absolute? Yes, just as the right to think is an absolute. Are there no exceptions? None whatever. Has not society the right to protect itself against noxious ideas? No. Oliver Wendell Holmes once said, "Noxious ideas are like champagne; expose them to the air and they fall flat." Who can be certain of what is the truth unless all views are heard?

In my practice of law, particularly in those cases where the liberties of people are at issue, I have learned that the course of justice is not always straight and swift. For what I have seen has convinced me that men are progressing. I believe that it is our time-tested democratic institutions which make this progress possible. For this reason, I am against anything which serves to weaken those institutions. I'm against congressional investigations into men's opinions. I'm against loyalty oaths. I'm against guilt by association. I believe that no man should lose his reputation, his liberty, or his property, except by judgment of court after fair trial according to Anglo-Saxon procedure.

Freedom is practical, as well as an ideological value. As long as men have the right freely to persuade and secretly to vote, we have a method of bringing about changes in our society, no matter how radical, without force or violence. Nor is it a matter of chance that the most prosperous and progressive countries in the world are, likewise, the freest.

Because I am unswervingly determined to help keep America free and secure, I derive the deepest satisfaction in doing everything I can to preserve and enlarge those liberties which have made our country great. If my efforts meet with any success, I think I will have reason to feel that I have been privileged to serve what I believe in, in the way that I know best.

Arthur Garfield Hays *was general counsel for the American Civil Liberties Union for thirty years. Among his many cases, Hays served as a defense attorney at the Scopes trial (along with Clarence Darrow), the Sacco and Vanzetti trial, and the Scottsboro Nine trial.*

Our Noble, Essential Decency

Robert Heinlein

I AM NOT GOING TO TALK ABOUT RELIGIOUS BELIEFS but about matters so obvious that it has gone out of style to mention them. I believe in my neighbors. I know their faults, and I know that their virtues far outweigh their faults.

Take Father Michael, down our road a piece. I'm not of his creed, but I know that goodness and charity and loving kindness shine in his daily actions. I believe in Father Mike. If I'm in trouble, I'll go to him. My next door neighbor's a veterinary doctor. Doc will get out of bed after a hard day to help a stray cat—no fee, no prospect of a fee. I believe in Doc.

I believe in my townspeople. You can knock on any door in our town, say "I'm hungry," and you'll be fed. Our town is no exception. I found the same ready charity everywhere. For the one who says, "The heck with you, I've got mine," there are a hundred, a thousand, who will say, "Sure pal, sit down." I know that despite all warnings against hitchhikers, I can step to the highway, thumb for a ride, and in a few minutes a car or a truck will stop and someone will say, "Climb in Mack. How far you going?"

I believe in my fellow citizens. Our headlines are splashed with crime. Yet for every criminal, there are ten thousand honest, decent, kindly men. If it were not so, no child would live to grow up. Business could not go on from day to day. Decency is not news. It is buried in the obituaries, but it is a force stronger than crime.

I believe in the patient gallantry of nurses, in the tedious sacrifices of teachers. I believe in the unseen and unending fight against desperate odds that goes on quietly in almost every home in the land. I believe in the honest craft of workmen. Take a look around you. There never were enough bosses to check up on all that work. From Independence Hall to the Grand Coulee Dam, these things were built level and square by craftsmen who were honest in their bones.

I believe that almost all politicians are honest. For every bribed alderman, there are hundreds of politicians—low paid or not paid at all—doing their level best without thanks or glory to make our system work. If this were not true, we would never have gotten past the Thirteen Colonies.

I believe in Rodger Young. You and I are free today because of endless unnamed heroes from Valley Forge to the Yalu River. I believe in—I am proud to belong to—the United States. Despite shortcomings—from lynchings, to bad faith in high places—our nation has had the most decent and kindly internal practices and foreign policies to be found anywhere in history.

And finally, I believe in my whole race—yellow, white, black, red, brown—in the honesty, courage, intelligence, durability, and goodness of the overwhelming majority of my brothers and sisters everywhere on this planet. I am proud to be a human being. I believe that we have come this far by the skin of our teeth—that we always make it just for the skin of our teeth—but that we will always make it, survive, endure.

I believe that this hairless embryo with the aching oversized braincase and the opposable thumb—this animal barely up from the apes—will endure, will endure longer than his home planet, will spread out to the other planets—to the stars and beyond—carrying with him his honesty, his insatiable curiosity, his unlimited courage, and his noble essential decency. This I believe with all my heart.

ROBERT A. HEINLEIN *won four Hugo Awards during his fifty-year career as a science fiction writer. Born and raised in Missouri, he graduated from the U.S. Naval Academy in 1929 and did aeronautical engineering for the Navy during World War II. Heinlein's books include* Starship Troopers *and* Stranger in a Strange Land.

Do You Know Your Special Talent?

ANNE HEYWOOD

WHAT I AM ABOUT TO SAY may appear to be plugging my own business, but it's what I know best—and I believe it deeply and sincerely. I believe that every human being has a talent—something that he can do better than anyone else. And I believe that the distinction between so-called "creative" talents and ordinary run-of-the-mill talents is an unnecessary and a man-made distinction. I have known exterminators and typists, waitresses and machinists whose creative joy and self-fulfillment in their work could not be surpassed by Shakespeare's or Einstein's.

When I was in my teens, I read a quotation from Thomas Carlyle: "Blessed is he who has found his work. Let him ask no other blessedness." At the time I thought that was a pretty grim remark, but I know now that Mr. Carlyle was right. When you find the thing that you can do better than anything else in the world, then all the wonderful byproducts fall in line: financial security, happy personal relationships, peace of mind. I believe that until you find it, your search for the byproducts will be in vain.

I also believe that in the process of searching, no experience is ever wasted, unless we allow ourselves to run out of hope. In my own case, I had thirty-four different jobs before I found the right one. Many of those jobs were heartbreakingly difficult. A few of them involved working with unscrupulous and horribly unpleasant people. Yet, in looking back, I can see that the most unpleasant of those jobs, in many cases, gave me the biggest dividends—the most valuable preparation for my proper life work.

And I have seen this happen in the destinies of hundreds of people. Periods which they thought were hopeless, dark, and of no possible practical value have turned out to be the most priceless experience they ever had. I know a girl who is a famous package designer for American Industry. She was just given a promotion for which she competed with six well-qualified designers. Her past, like all of ours, had its good times and its bad times. One of the worst of the bad times was a period when she lost her husband and was left with two small children to support. She took a clerking job in a grocery store because her apartment was on the floor above it and between customers she could run up and keep an eye on the babies.

It was a two-year period of great despair, during which she was constantly on the verge of suicide. Yet the other day when she told me of her promotion to the top package design job, she exclaimed in astonishment, "And do you know that the single factor which swung it in my favor was that I alone had over-the-counter experience with the customers who buy our packaged foods!"

When people talk about the sweet uses of adversity, I think they unduly stress a grim and kind of hopeless resignation, a conviction that, like unpleasant medicine, it's somehow "good for us." But I think it's much more than that. I know that the unhappy periods of our lives offer us concrete and useful plus-values, chief among them a heightened understanding and compassion for others. We may not see it at the time, we may consider the experience entirely wasted but, as Emerson says, "The years teach much which the days never know."

Iowa native ANNE HEYWOOD *held thirty-four different jobs before founding the Career Changing Clinic in New York City to help service men and women returning from World War II find work. Heywood was a syndicated columnist and the author of* There Is a Right Job for Every Woman.

A New Birth of Freedom

MAXIMILIAN HODDER

TO STATE CLEARLY AND HONESTLY ONE'S BELIEFS in a few hundred words is a large order in any man's language, particularly so if one has been a victim of a number of very personal tragedies.

Ever since my adolescent mind began to comprehend the complexities of our daily life, I looked upon a human being as a personification of that great unknown with a very specific mission on earth to fulfill. I looked for perfection, for love, and understanding. I believe in human being.

Then, one day from the world of a carefree, happy life of a young, up-and-coming writer/director in prewar Poland, I was thrown into the Nazis' and, later, communists' world of hatred, tyranny, murder, and destruction. Human being ceased to be what I believed it was destined for, and I became the raw material for a soap factory, an implement in a five-year plan, or a guinea pig in a biological laboratory. I lost my country and my family, and my belief in human being was crushed mercilessly. I became bitter and cynical.

Then came the third and, to me perhaps, the most significant period of my life so far, here in America. From the moment the immigration officer at LaGuardia Airport shook my hand and wished me good luck, I again began to see the sunnier side of life. I have made true friends and they have proven themselves when I needed them most. Food and clothing for victims of floods, a group of GIs adopting an orphan and sending him to school, neighbors building a new home for a victim of fire, Community Chest, Cancer Fund, Salvation Army, Alcoholics Anonymous, and a thousand other such acts or associations, all voluntary, collective or individual, left an indelible mark on me. It gave me a new lease on life. I again believe in mankind.

I now remember not only the days when people were chased from houses of worship with guns, but also those poor Russians who traded for food their most treasured possessions, but kept the holy icons. I now think not only of those who killed, but also of the kind Russian peasants who met our convoy to Siberia and, in spite of guys who chased them away, tried to share with us corned beef, a piece of bread, perhaps their last one. I also think of those gun-starved wretches who, after years of unendurable exploitation in forced labor camps, still had enough humanness left in them to sing or even joke occasionally.

I now, again, believe there is more good than evil; more of those who create, or wish to create, than those who destroy; more of those who love than those who hate. I firmly believe in an inalienable right of the individual to live the life of his choice, his right to work or rest, smile or cry, succeed or fail, pray or play.

The great Polish poet Adam Mickiewicz said, "The nectar of life is sweet only when shared with others." I therefore also believe that it is my duty to contribute, in whatever way I can, to the present struggle to bring hope to those still oppressed, so that, as a great American once said, "They also may, under God, have a new birth of freedom."

Director MAXIMILIAN HODDER *worked in the movie industries of Eastern Europe. While serving in the Polish Army during World War II, he was captured by the Soviets but managed to escape and went on to join the Royal Air Force. Hodder came to the United States in 1949 to work in Hollywood.*

The Light of a Brighter Day

~~~~

HELEN KELLER

I CHOOSE FOR MY SUBJECT FAITH wrought into life apart from creed or dogma. By faith, I mean a vision of good one cherishes and the enthusiasm that pushes one to seek its fulfillment, regardless of obstacles. Faith is a dynamic power that breaks the chain of routine, and gives a new, fine turn to old commonplaces. Faith reinvigorates the will, enriches the affections, and awakens a sense of creativeness. Active faith knows no fear, and it is a safeguard to me against cynicism and despair.

After all, faith is not one thing or two or three things. It is an indivisible totality of beliefs that inspire me. Belief in God as infinite goodwill and all-seeing Wisdom, whose everlasting arms sustain me walking on the sea of life. Trust in my fellow men, wonder at their fundamental goodness, and confidence that after this night of sorrow and oppression, they will rise up strong and beautiful in the glory of morning. Reverence for the beauty and preciousness of the earth and a sense of responsibility to do what I can to make it a habitation of health and plenty for all men. Faith in immortality because it renders less bitter the separation from those I have loved and lost—and because it will free me from unnatural limitations and unfold still more faculties I have in joyous activity.

Even if my vital spark should be blown out, I believe that I should behave with courageous dignity in the presence of fate and strive to be a worthy companion of the beautiful, the good, and the true. But fate has its master in the faith of those who surmount it, and limitation has its limits for those who, though disillusioned, live greatly.

It was a terrible blow to my faith when I learned that millions of my fellow creatures must labor all their days for food and shelter, bear the most crushing burdens, and die without having known the joy of living. My security vanished forever, and I have never regained the radiant belief of my young years that earth is a happy home and hearth for the majority of mankind. But faith is a state of mind. The believer is not soon disheartened. If he is turned out of his shelter, he builds up a house that the winds of the earth cannot destroy.

When I think of the suffering and famine, and the

continued slaughter of men, my spirit bleeds. But the thought comes to me that, like the little deaf, dumb, and blind child I once was, mankind is growing out of the darkness of ignorance and hate into the light of a brighter day.

As an infant, HELEN KELLER was struck by a fever that left her deaf and blind. But with the guidance of her teacher, Anne Sullivan, she learned to communicate through the eyes and ears of others. After graduating from Radcliffe College, Keller became a renowned author, activist, and lecturer.

Freedom from Fear

⟋⟋⟋⟍

Phyllis Kirk

If it is accepted that the life span of the human being of our time averages approximately seventy-five years, I will, in a short while, reach the end of what may be the first third of my life. In the course of deliberately walking into the past of myself I've made many discoveries, some of them encouraging, even happy ones. But it disturbs me deeply to also discover that I've spent so much of this first portion of my life being afraid of almost everything and that I have spent so much of the remaining time in learning the myriad tricks there are by which one may hide one's fear from others. It disturbs me to realize that in the seemingly harmless act of deluding others into believing me to be unafraid, I have also deluded myself.

The sudden awareness of the enormous part which fear has played in my living has been particularly shocking to me because I've always thought that I loved life in its fullest sense of loving it as I could, and I've always thought that I believed intensely in the experiment of living it. I believe that when we permit ourselves to fear, we negate the chance we are each given to contribute through the unique patterns of our respective lives to the meaning and validity of all life. I believe that in merely being alive we have a tremendous responsibility, and that the responsibility is not only to our separate selves but to one another.

I believe it is in fear that we commit the crimes of intolerance and prejudice and what seems to me to be perhaps the saddest, most grave crime of all, our resistance to change. Afraid, we fail to see that the change is the natural and good fruit of knowledge and growth. We cling to the familiar because it is familiar and seems, therefore, to be secure. We butcher the unfamiliar and slaughter justice with the same stroke. Frightened, we seek love only for ourselves and forget to search for love in ourselves.

In fear, we restrict the membership and close the doors of our churches. We court the man who is willing to chant the service least alien to ours. In fear, we make the manner of worship and the name by which a man identifies his god more important than a man's knowledge of his need, and his striving for faith and a power of good greater than himself.

As children we are taught the visionless prejudices of our parents. We are taught and we, in turn, teach our children perhaps not the same prejudices, but each of them common to one another, for they are born and sustained in fear. I want a child of my own, and I want him to be unafraid. I believe that for him, freedom from fear can have its beginning now in me because I feel so strongly that in the living of my life, I have a responsibility to all life. Because of the child not yet conceived in me, I believe I must grow enough today to face yesterday's mistakes.

I believe tomorrow is hopeful and that if I am to recognize tomorrow as promising, I must not fear its being different from today. I believe I must try with all I know—and without fear of all I don't know—to never really be afraid again. Each of us has known guilt; each of us is alone. I believe that guilty and alone, we are all here together.

Actress PHYLLIS KIRK *starred with Vincent Price in the horror film* House of Wax *and with Peter Lawford in* The Thin Man *television series. She later worked in public relations at CBS. Throughout her career, Kirk was active in various social and civil liberties causes.*

Devotion to the Common Good

———

Mrs. John G. Lee

I THINK THE MOST PROFOUND INFLUENCE IN MY LIFE was my father. He was an inventor and a scientist with a most inquisitive mind. He loved and was greatly stimulated by the beauty and the design he found in nature. He believed in people and was himself a completely honest person. His sense of humor was keen though kindly, and his energy was inexhaustible. Once he was asked how he got the idea for the Maxim Silencer. He answered, "By watching the way water behaved when it went down a drain."

This simple statement opened up for me a whole realm of ideas which led to a firm belief that human intelligence need recognize no bounds, that through the use of our

intelligence we will move progressively closer to an understanding of man and of the universe around us, that this
knowledge will bring a closer harmony between man and his
surroundings, and that this way lies the chance to make the
world a better place to live in.

Then I remember sitting with him on the deck of his
boat one night in early September. We were anchored in a
secluded cove. The breeze was light and very salty. We could
hear across a little strip of land the pounding of the surf.
The stars were brilliant and every now and then a shooting
star would streak across the sky. He was deeply interested in
astronomy and he led my mind into unforgettable specula-
tion as we explored the grandeur of that night. I think from
this I came to understand that there must be law and order
in our universe. There is design. Man can observe, he can
learn to understand, he can apply. The secret is to apply in
the interests of the common good, not for one or for a few,
not to destroy, but to build for all peoples.

My mother and father each had an acute social conscience.
They believed that because good fortune had endowed them
with better than average opportunity, they had a duty to perform in their communities. From this, no doubt, came my
own conviction that I must give more than I receive and that a
satisfactory life must be measured by its usefulness to others.

I remember the excitement engendered by the

conversation in our home. All kinds of ideas were explored, all sorts of prejudices were challenged, penetrating minds were brought to bear on every problem of the day. I learned that each one of us has a right to his own beliefs, that prejudice perverts truth, and that violence in the long run gains us nothing. From this understanding I moved into the belief that people everywhere must learn how to work together for the common purpose of the betterment of mankind.

I believe one of the greatest ideas of all times, one that is a compelling moral force, is the concept of the dignity and worth of the human individual. From this idea there develops a sense of devotion to the common good.

I believe that if we pull these rather simple but fundamental things together and tie them up with honesty and truth, there are no visible limits to the heights to which mankind can rise.

MRS. JOHN G. (PERCY) LEE *served four terms as the national president of the League of Women Voters from 1950 to 1958. The daughter of the inventor of the Maxim gun silencer, Lee passed up college to marry at age nineteen and raise a family.*

The Only Way to Make a Friend

Herbert Lehman

So many things affect a man's philosophy and his life that I find it difficult to put into words my personal beliefs. I hesitate to speak of them publicly for fear of giving the appearance of preaching.

Two convictions, however, I believe have more than any others influenced my thinking both in private and in public life.

First, commonplace as it may sound, I am convinced that what we get out of life is in direct proportion to what we put into it. Second, I must respect the opinions of others even if I disagree with them.

Throughout my long and rather busy career, I have always

held firmly to the belief that I owe life as much as it owes to me. If that philosophy is sound, and I believe that it is, it applies, I hope, to all of my activities—to my home, to my daily work, to my politics and, above all things, to my relationships to others.

Life is not a one-way street. What I do, what I say, even what I think, inevitably has a direct effect on my relationships with others. I am certain that in the degree that my attitude towards others has given convincing proof of loyalty, sincerity, honesty, courtesy, and fairness, I have encouraged in others the same attitude towards me. Respect begets respect, suspicion begets suspicion, hate begets hate. It has been well said that "The only way to have a friend is to be one."

None of the blessings of our great American heritage of civil liberties is self-executing. To make effective such things as brotherhood, kindliness, sympathy, human decency, the freedom of opportunity, the very preciousness of life—to make these things real requires respect and constant vigilance. This is the core of my American Faith.

As I have said, I believe I must help to safeguard to all men free expression of their views even though I may be in disagreement with them. I must listen to and study responsible views; sometimes I will learn much from them. No individual and no nation has a monopoly of wisdom or talent. When an individual or a nation becomes self-satisfied or complacent, it is time, I believe, to be deeply concerned. He who closes his ears to the views of others shows little confidence in the integrity of his own views.

There can be no question with regard to the inherent rights of Americans to enjoy equal economic opportunity in every field, to secure decent living conditions, adequate provision for the moral and spiritual development of their children, and free association with their fellow men as equals under the law and equals in the sight of God. These rights can be safeguarded and advanced only where men may think and speak freely. I reject a fundamental principle of democracy if I seek to prevent a fellow citizen of different background from fully expressing his thoughts on any subject. I have tried to express a few of my own thoughts on this subject which is very close to me. I think that we will have good reason for optimism about the future of the American ideal as long as men can and will say, without fear, what they believe.

HERBERT H. LEHMAN *was a partner in the Lehman Brothers investment banking firm. He served in the Army during World War I, rising to the rank of colonel. Lehman was Governor of New York from 1933 to 1942 and served as a U.S. Senator from 1949 until 1957.*

Twice I Sought Death

~~~~~

Marty Mann

I AM AN ALCOHOLIC—one of the fortunate ones who found the road to recovery. That was thirteen years ago, but I haven't forgotten. I remember what it was like to be hopelessly in the grip of the vicious disease of alcoholism, not knowing what was wrong with me. I remember my desperate search for help. Failing to find it, I remember my inner despair—my outer defiance.

I remember the arrogance and pride with which I faced the non-understanding world, in spite of my terrible hidden fears—my fear of life and my fear of death. At times I feared life so much more than death that twice I sought death. Suicide seemed a welcome release from a terror and agony past bearing.

How grateful I am now that I didn't succeed. But I believed in nothing, then. Not in myself, nor in anything outside myself. I was walled in with my suffering—alone and, I thought, forsaken.

But I wasn't forsaken, of course. No one is, really. I seemed to suffer alone, but I believe now that I was never alone—that none of us are. I believe, too, that I was never given more to bear than I could endure, but rather that my suffering was necessary, for me. I believe it may well have taken that much suffering, in my case, to break down my wall of self, to crush my arrogance and pride, to let me seek and accept the help that was there.

For in the depths of my suffering I came to believe. To believe that there was a Power greater than myself that could help me. To believe that because of that Power—God—there was hope and help for me.

I found my help through people—doctors whose vocation it is to deal with suffering, and other human beings who had suffered like myself. In the depths of my personal abyss I received understanding and kindness and help from many individuals. People, I learned, can be very kind. I came to believe deeply in this—in people and the good that is in them.

I came to realize that suffering is universal. It lies behind much apparent harshness and irritability, many of the careless, even cruel, words and acts which make our daily lives difficult so much of the time. I learned that if I could understand this, I might not react so often with anger or hurt. And if I learned to react to difficult behavior with understanding and sympathy, I might help to bring about a change in that behavior. My suffering helped me to know things.

I do not believe that everyone should suffer. But I do believe that suffering can be good, and even necessary, if—and only if—one learns to accept that suffering as part of one's essential learning process, and then to use it to help oneself and one's fellow sufferers.

Don't we all endure suffering, one way or another? This fact gives me a deep sense of kinship with other people and a consequent desire to help others in any and every way I can.

It is this belief that underlies my work, for alcoholism is the area in which I feel best fitted, through my own experience, to help others. And I believe that trying to help my fellow men is one of the straightest roads to spiritual growth. It is a road everyone can take. One doesn't have to be beautiful or gifted or rich or powerful, in order to offer a helping hand to one's fellow sufferers. And I believe that one can walk with God by doing just that.

MARTY MANN *was the first woman to join Alcoholics Anonymous. She founded the National Committee on Alcoholism in 1944, now known as the National Council on Alcoholism and Drug Dependence (NCADD). Born into a wealthy Chicago family, Mann worked as a magazine editor, art critic, and photographer.*

Why I Close My Restaurant

George Mardikian

Every Christmas eve, I close my restaurant to the public. My wife and I become the hired help to serve our employees. We try to give them the finest Christmas repast. This exchange of roles is symbolic. This is an ancient Armenian custom we have introduced into our American life.

Each national group has brought something of its heritage in the form of thousands of different customs, which have become integral parts of life in this country. I believe that true humility is a basic need of mankind today. Why do I believe this? Aside from the fact that Jesus Christ taught it, my own experiences seem to me a living testimony of its truth.

As a young man in my native Armenia, I was organizing

boy scout troops when the Turks and the Russians invaded the Republic of Armenia. I was captured and thrown into prison. I nearly starved to death in this time of crisis. An older and wiser inmate said to me, "Don't lose hope." He was right, for some American friends in the Near East Relief helped me to escape. They used the ruse of telling my captors that I was an American. I became an American before I became an American.

Eventually, I was able to work my way to the United States. Here I was, a humble immigrant boy crossing the Atlantic to a country that seemed to answer all my prayers for happiness and freedom. My feelings when I first saw the Statue of Liberty cannot be described. Even today, when I pass it on my frequent trips to Europe, a feeling—something like reverence—comes over me.

When I entered the shower baths at Ellis Island, I found plenty of soap and water. I used them freely because it seemed to me that I was washing away all the hatreds and prejudices of the old world. As I stepped out of the shower and came face to face with a guard in uniform, he actually smiled at me. The smile of a stranger may seem to be a fleeting, insignificant moment to others, but I remember it vividly because it set the mood for my new life. It was perhaps an omen of the joy and friendship I was to find about me.

When I first arrived, I spoke very little English and

had practically no money. But I did have enthusiasm, the will to work, and bright hopes for a new life ahead. I got on the westbound train for San Francisco. Everywhere I went strangers were willing to help, and I felt very humble.

This wonderful land has been good to me. It has given me friends by the hundreds in all walks of life. I believe that in this society where love and mutual respect are fostered and encouraged, I must do more than contribute my share towards the material and the spiritual well being of all. I believe that friendship, which grows out of love and true humility, is the most important thing in life.

GEORGE MARDIKIAN's *first job in America was washing dishes in a San Francisco cafeteria; he eventually bought the place and built it into a renowned restaurant. For his work to improve food service for combat troops in Korea, Mardikian was awarded the Medal of Freedom, the highest civilian award an American can receive.*

The Courage to Change the Things I Can

HARRY S. McALPIN

BASIC IN MY LIFE HAVE BEEN THESE BELIEFS: that there are some things for which I am not responsible, some I cannot change, and some I can. Around recognition and acceptance of these facts, I have tried to build a philosophy by which to live in our complex society.

Forty-six years ago I was born a Negro in America. For this, of course, I was not responsible, though I am proud of it. I have traveled around the world and have learned from experience that I would rather be an American, with an inalienable right to fight against discriminations and prejudices and injustices, than to be any other nationality with a pseudo-equality, in slavery to the state, unable or afraid to express or even think my dislikes or disagreements, as is the case in Russia and other communist-controlled countries.

I had a father who regrettably died when I was fifteen years old and a senior in high school. He was a man of great principle. He abhorred injustice. He believed, in spite of the handicaps he suffered because of his color, that all men were created equal in the sight of God, and that included him and me. He instilled me with his beliefs. To live by these beliefs, I have found it necessary to develop patience, to build courage, to pray for wisdom. But despite my fervent prayers, I find it is not always easy to live up to my creed.

The complexities of modern day living—particularly as I must face them day to day as a Negro in America— often put my creed to test. It takes a great deal of patience to accept the customs of some sections and communities, to try to fit into the crossword puzzle of living the illogic of a practice that will permit me to ride on the public busses without segregation and seating, but deny me the right to rent a private room to myself in a hotel; or the illogic of a practice which will accept me as a chauffeur for the rich who can afford it, but deny me the opportunity of driving one of the public busses I may ride indiscriminately; or the illogic of a practice which will accept me and require me to fight on the same battlefield but deny me the right to ride in the same coach on a train.

It takes a great deal of courage to put principles of right and justice ahead of economic welfare and well being, to stand up and challenge established and accepted practices, which amount to arbitrary exercise of power by petty politicians in office or by the police. Trying to live up to my beliefs often has subjected me to both praise and criticism. How wise I have been in my choices may be known only to God. I firmly believe, however, that as an American, as a man, and as a Christian, I have been strengthened, and life about me has been made better by the steel hardening fires through which my creed and my faith have carried me.

I shall continue to pray, therefore, a prayer I learned in the distant past, which I now count as my own: "God, give me serenity to accept the things I cannot change, courage to change the things I can, and wisdom to know the difference."

HARRY S. MCALPIN *was the first African-American reporter credentialed to the White House, where he covered Presidents Roosevelt and Truman for fifty-one black newspapers. He was also a Navy war correspondent and spokesman for the Department of Agriculture. Later, McAlpin practiced law in Louisville, Kentucky.*

A New Control of Destiny

MARGARET MEAD

CHILDREN USED TO PLAY A GAME of pointing at someone, suddenly saying, "What are you?" Some people answered by saying, "I am a human being," or by nationality, or by religion. When this question was put to me by a new generation of children, I answered, "an anthropologist." Anthropology is the study of whole ways of life, to which one must be completely committed, all the time. So that when I speak of what I believe as a person, I cannot separate this from what I believe as an anthropologist.

I believe that to understand human beings it is necessary to think of them as part of the whole living world. Our essential humanity depends not only on the complex biological structure which has been developed through the ages from very simple beginnings, but also upon the great social inventions which have been made by human beings, perpetuated by human beings and, in turn, give human beings their stature as builders, thinkers, statesmen, artists, seers, and prophets.

I believe that each of these great inventions—language, the family, the use of tools, government, science, art, and philosophy—has the quality of so combining the potentialities of every human temperament, that each can be learned and perpetuated by any group of human beings, regardless of race, and regardless of the type of civilization within which their progenitors lived, so that a newborn infant from the most primitive tribe in New Guinea is as intrinsically capable of graduation from Harvard, or writing a sonnet, or inventing a new form of radar as an infant born on Beacon Hill.

But I believe, also, that once a child has been reared in New Guinea or Boston or Leningrad or Tibet, he embodies the culture within which he is reared and differs from those who are reared elsewhere so deeply that only by understanding these differences can we reach an awareness which will give us a new control over our human destiny.

I believe that human nature is neither intrinsically good nor intrinsically evil, but individuals are born with different combinations of innate potentialities and that it will depend upon how they are reared—to trust and love and experiment and create, or to fear and hate and conform— what kind of human beings they can become. I believe that we have not even begun to tap human potentialities and that by continuing humble but persistent study of human behavior, we can learn consciously to create civilizations within which an increasing proportion of human beings will realize more of what they have it in them to be.

I believe that human life is given meaning through the relationship which the individual's conscious goals have to the civilization, period, and country within which one lives. At times, the task may be to fence a wilderness, to bridge a river, or rear sons to perpetuate a young colony. Today, it means taking upon ourselves the task of creating one world in such a way that we both keep the future safe and leave the future free.

Anthropologist MARGARET MEAD *spent many years in Polynesia studying native cultures there. She also worked as an associate curator at the American Museum of Natural History, a professor at Columbia University, and a president of the American Association for the Advancement of Science.*

All Men Are My Brothers

‿◠

James Michener

I believe that all men are brothers. I really believe that every man on this earth is my brother. He has a soul like mine, the ability to understand friendship, the capacity to create beauty. In all the continents of this world, I have met such men. In the most savage jungles of New Guinea, I have met my brother, and in Tokyo, I have seen him clearly walking before me.

In my brother's house, I have lived without fear. Once in the wildest part of Guadalcanal I had to spend some days with men who still lived and thought in the old stone age, but we got along together fine. In the South Pacific, on remote islands, I have sailed and fished with brown men who were in every respect the same as I.

Around the world I have lived with my brothers and nothing has kept me from knowing men like myself wherever I went. Language has been no barrier, for once in India, I lived for several days with villagers who didn't know a word of English. I can't remember exactly how we got along, but the fact that I couldn't speak their language was no hindrance. Differences in social custom never kept me from getting to know and like savage Melanesians in the New Hebrides. They ate roast dog, and I ate Army spam, and if we had wanted to emphasize differences, I am sure each of us could have concluded the other was nuts. But we stressed similarities and, so long as I could snatch a Navy blanket for them now and then, we had a fine old time with no words spoken.

It was in these islands that I met a beat-up, shameless old Tonkinese woman. She would buy or sell anything, and in time we became fast friends and I used to sit with her, knowing not a word of her curious language, and we talked for hours. She knew only half a dozen of the vilest English obscenities, but she had the most extraordinary love of human beings and the most infectious sense of this world's crazy comedy. She was of my blood, and I wish I could see her now.

I believe it was only fortunate experience that enabled me to travel among my brothers and to live with them. Therefore

I do not believe it is my duty to preach to other people and insist that they also accept all men as their true and immediate brothers. These things come slow. Sometimes it takes lucky breaks to open our eyes. For example, if I had never known this wonderful old Tonkinese woman, I might not now think of all Chinese as my brothers. I had to learn, as I believe the world will one day learn. Until such time as experience proves to all of us the essential brotherhood of man, I am not going to preach or scream or rant.

But if I am tolerant of other men's prejudices, I must insist that they be tolerant of me. To my home in rural Pennsylvania come brown men and yellow men and black men from around the world. In their countries I lived and ate with them. In my country they shall live and eat with me. Until the day I die, my home must be free to receive these travelers and it never seems so big a home or so much a place of love as when some man from India or Japan or Mexico or Tahiti or Fiji shares it with me. For on those happy days, it reminds me of the wonderful affection I have known throughout the world.

I believe that all men are my brothers. I know it when I see them sharing my home.

JAMES A. MICHENER *wrote his Pulitzer Prize–winning novel* Tales of the South Pacific *during his naval service in World War II after seeking a transfer from a desk job in Washington to the Pacific theater. Michener's literary career spanned fifty years and forty books.*

Thy Will Be Done

⟶

ROBBINS MILBANK

I BELIEVE IT IS VERY EASY to build God in your own image and very hard to rebuild Him when you crumble. I was born to see and experience the love of God. I saw Him in my father, whose kindness and wisdom led me through a thousand anguishes of youth. I saw Him in my wife—especially in her. I told my father about her when I was nine years old. "We're going to marry," I said.

He smiled. "I'm glad you feel like telling me. I hope you'll always want to tell me things like this."

For many years I was rich, seeing and loving and touching these children of God. I knew what I believed, because I believed in them and they in me.

They died. First my father. Then my wife. Why do I still arrange my deskwork in neat piles? Why do I straighten a piece of furniture? Why do I try to arrive at appointments a minute early? Why do I lie down to sleep or get up in the morning? Have you ever wandered through an empty house looking for a purpose? You do a lot of little things automatically.

I'd like to talk about my house. It talks to me quietly in the night of the love it still shares, of the garden that still surrounds it, of the laughter of our children and grandchildren and our pride in them. I lie on my bed pulling words around, trying to understand their meaning. Words like "I believe."

This I know: I believe in the Lord's Prayer, all of it, but particularly where it says "thy will be done." For me, that's one clear channel to God. That one belief, "thy will be done," carries me through each act of each day. It teaches me to live with all that is given me and to live without what is taken away. It rescues me from the idea that happiness for myself is either important or desirable. But it doesn't at all destroy happiness as a gift I can give, miraculously, from an empty vessel.

I believe I'm held here in trust, that I have no right to violate that trust through negation, no right to turn inward or away from people or jobs I can do. What if I do start through habit and finish in a half dream? The belief suffices: "Thy will be done."

I believe there is nothing passive yielding my will to

God's. It keeps me very busy using the brain He gave me to study fields that need plowing; using the heart He gave me to remember these fields belong to His people; using the faith He gave me to pass up self-satisfaction for doing something I want to do anyway.

I noticed something: you may notice something quite wonderful in most everybody you meet, even in those who annoy you or frighten you. But each, in his way, is truth— neither to be rejected nor run from. If you believe "thy will be done," there is less temptation to run away from yourself. You can't escape, anyway.

A Princeton graduate and son of a prominent New England family, ROBBINS MILBANK *worked as a logger in British Columbia for six years. He later moved into advertising, becoming a vice president at McCann-Erickson, and wrote docu-dramas for television.*

Ethical Living and Desirable Ends

—◦

ARTHUR E. MORGAN

THE GREATEST INNER STRUGGLE OF MY LIFE was in my teens over whether to hold without question the faiths of the fathers or to freely inquire. Years of deep concern convinced me that free inquiry is more than a right, it is a duty. Truly free inquiry is possible only with right living. Loose or self-centered living warps thinking to justify itself.

Since where one does not doubt, he does not really inquire, unquestioning belief may miss the larger truth. I will not believe just because it gives me comfort. Where honest inquiry does not lead to assurance, I admit, I do not know. I respect the convictions of others, asking only that they claim no monopoly of truth. Here are some slowly won conclusions.

Every living thing has an inner urge to perfection, according to its type. Faith, hope, aspiration—inherent in life itself—are older, stronger, deeper than any creed. Man is part of nature. In him, this aspiration becomes conscious search for value. Life has traveled a long hard road. Unnumbered species have lost the way and become extinct. Can man squander his inheritance, yet survive? Unsparing inquiry leaves me faith that if he would do his reasonable best, he probably will succeed in his great quest.

Were success foreordained, how I live would not change the prospect. If, as seems to me, human life is a real adventure with possibility of failure as well as of success, then sincere purposeful living may affect the outcome. The margin of probability of full success in the human adventure may not be great. Take a semi-fanciful case: Suppose atomic war, should it occur, might destroy humanity. Whether mutual confidence grows fast enough to prevent such war may depend partly on how I help build mutual trust, how fully and wisely I share with those less fortunate, how completely I pursue the good life as a whole, not just my own.

There probably are less obvious but greater dangers than atomic war. Biological evolution works very slowly. For instance, the impulse to revenge—widespread in men and animals—is baneful to civilized life. Many thousand years probably would pass before that impulse would be weeded out by biological selection. Insight and intelligence counsel:

Forgive your enemies. Thus ethical living moves directly toward desirable ends while biological evolution blindly fumbles. Ethics grows with experience, insight, and critical appraisal.

Of numberless possible and desirable goals, I am not sure which are best. But there are ways of living which I am sure will lead toward the best. These include goodwill and sincerity, doing as I would be done by, being honest with myself. My opportunity—my duty—is loyalty to the quest of life for values. To live as a dilettante, or for personal ends, is betrayal. Where one's treasure is, there will his heart be also. As I train my desires so that my treasure is the good of life as a whole, I become immune to the despair which may follow failure of lesser hopes.

ARTHUR E. MORGAN *was a self-taught civil engineer, as well as an educator, a writer of more than twenty books, and a labor arbiter. He served as the first chairman of the Tennessee Valley Authority and as president of Antioch College in Ohio.*

How to Refill an Empty Life

—◦—

ALBERT J. NESBITT

ONE DAY ABOUT FIFTEEN YEARS AGO I suddenly came face to face with myself and realized there was something quite empty about my life. My friends and associates perhaps didn't see it. By the generally accepted standards, I was "successful," I was head of a prosperous manufacturing concern and led what is usually referred to as an "active" life, both socially and in business. But it didn't seem to me to be adding up to anything. I was going around in circles. I worked hard, played hard, and pretty soon I discovered I was hitting the highballs harder than I needed. I wasn't a candidate for Alcoholics Anonymous, but to be honest with myself I had to admit I was drinking more than was good for me. It may have been out of sheer boredom.

I began to wonder what to do. It occurred to me that I might have gotten myself too tightly wrapped up in my job, to the sacrifice of the basic but non-materialistic values of life. It struck me abruptly that I was being quite selfish, that my major interest in people was in what they meant to me, what they represented as business contacts or employees, not what I might mean to them. I remembered that as my mother sent me to Sunday school as a boy and encouraged me to sing in the church choir, she used to tell me that the value of what she called a good Christian background was in having something to tie to. I put in a little thought recalling the Golden Rule and some of the other first principles of Christianity. I began to get interested in YMCA work.

It happened that just at this time we were having some bitter fights with the union at our plant. Then one day it occurred to me: What really is their point of view, and why? I began to see a basis for their suspicions, their often chip-on-shoulder point of view, and I determined to do something about it.

We endeavored to apply—literally apply—Christian principles to our dealing with employees, to practice, for example, something of the Golden Rule. The men's response, once they were convinced we were sincere, was remarkable. The effort has paid for its pains, and I don't mean in dollars.

I mean in dividends of human dignity, of a man's pride in his job and in the company, knowing that he is no longer just a cog but a live personal part of it and that it doesn't matter whether he belongs to a certain church or whether the pigmentation of his skin is light or dark.

But I can speak with most authority on how this change of attitude affected me and my personal outlook on life. Perhaps, again, many of my friends did not notice the difference.

But I noticed it. That feeling of emptiness, into which I was pouring cocktails out of boredom, was filling up instead with a purpose: to live a full life with an awareness and appreciation of other people. I do not pretend for a second that I have suddenly become a paragon. My faults are still legion and I know them.

But it seems to me better to have a little religion and practice it than think piously and do nothing about it. I feel better adjusted, more mature than I ever have in my life before. I have no fear. I say this not boastfully but in all humility. The actual application of Christian principles has changed my life.

ALBERT J. NESBITT *was president of the John J. Nesbitt Company, which manufactured heating and ventilating units. Among his many civic activities, Nesbitt served as the president of the Philadelphia YMCA and the Philadelphia Council of Churches.*

They Lived Their Faith

⟜⟞

CHARLES HENRY PARRISH

As I LOOK BACK, I have the growing conviction that much of what I now believe can be traced to my parents. My present attitudes seem to have resulted from an accumulation of many small and apparently insignificant childhood experiences. These beliefs I hold must have taken root early because as far back as I can remember, they were no different fundamentally from what they are now.

As the son of a Baptist minister, I have often wondered why my religious beliefs were not more strictly orthodox. Undoubtedly it was the sort of person my father was, rather than what he said in sermons or pamphlets that influenced me most. My father's private secretary was Catholic. It never seemed incongruous to me that he should bring back to her beads that had been blessed by Pope Pius X or that a large picture of the Pope should be prominently displayed in our home. Because of this memory, perhaps, the theological technicalities of doctrinal disputes leave me completely unmoved. I believe that every man must find out for himself, and that it does not really matter under whose auspices the search is made.

Nearly always, as I can remember, there were non-paying guests at our house. Uncomplainingly, my mother would do the necessary things to make them comfortable. Sometimes the persons who came were complete strangers. A gospel singer who had missed her train called up from the station and asked to be put up for the night. She stayed for three weeks. A stranded evangelist was with us for all of one winter. I do not recall that anyone was ever turned away. People in trouble inevitably came to my father for help. Although victimized many times, he was always ready to do whatever he could for the next person who asked his aid. He seemed not to think of himself. Yet, he enjoyed a moderate prosperity and his family never wanted for anything. It has thus become a part of me to believe that in the long run, I could never lose anything by helping other people.

The details of my father's early life have always been a source of inspiration for me. It was a life of struggle.

To the ordinary difficulties encountered was added the handicap of his racial origin. He had to fight continuously against racial intolerance. What has become increasingly significant for me was that he fought without bitterness. So far as I know, he never hated anybody. He must have believed in the essential goodness of people. I have come, gradually, to share this belief.

If I have stressed the importance of my father in determining my basic outlook on life, it is not to leave the impression that the influence of my mother has been negligible. It is, rather, that they were of one mind on the fundamental issues. My mother had varied outside interests, too, but her own family was the center of her loyalties. No sacrifice was too great for those she loved. Her devotion has had a profound influence in shaping my evaluations and beliefs.

These memories and impressions of my parents are the materials out of which my credo has been forged. Perhaps they would not have phrased it as I have. They might not have put it into words at all. They lived their faith. Its essence for me is couched on the belief that if I look always for the good in other people, I will surely catch a vision of God.

As a professor of sociology at the University of Louisville, CHARLES HENRY PARRISH *was the first African-American to be appointed to the faculty of a southern university. In addition to his teaching, Parrish was a part-time public relations consultant for the Domestic Life Insurance Company.*

I Quit Carrying a Gun

Robert B. Powers

For many years I searched for someone who could answer my questions. I looked everywhere—in faces and books. Lawrence of Arabia had some of the answers, so I read and re-read his *Seven Pillars of Wisdom* as well as his letters.

Everything about Lawrence made him more than a hero to me. He was almost a prophet. There was only one flaw. His latter years distressed me. Why should one of his brilliance, courage, and integrity have had to end his life in obscurity—yes, and anguish—as an enlisted man in the British Air Force?

One day I found myself talking about Lawrence. You know how it is, when you get started and can't stop? But finally, I ended with "Why, why did this have to happen to him?"

There was a long pause. Then a woman said, almost as if she were talking to herself, "His life among the Arabs—he must have known the *Koran*. There is a passage which Muslims believe are the words of God: 'And we desire to show favor to those who were brought low in the land, and to make them spiritual leaders among men, and to make them our heirs.'"

My question was answered. I was no longer troubled. That was seven years ago, and since then I have looked for answers, directions, in the Holy Books of all religions.

In Judaism I found a reverence I'd never known before for Law. And there, too, I became aware of the dramatic effect on my life of the words: "The Lord our God, the Lord is One."

Reading the Gospels with a new eye, I found the criterion—the reference point—for individual behavior and integrity. Whereas I had lived a violent life, I quit carrying a gun, accepting the relaxing concept of non-resistance. In the *Koran* I found the answers to group-living and the meaning of "Submission to the Will of God" in an active as well as a passive sense.

From the Zoroasterian writings—"Arise, 'tis dawn! Who riseth first comest first to paradise"—I found new zest for work and living. From Hinduism, I learned to "renounce the fruits of labor."

And from the Baha'i—"The earth is but one country and mankind its citizens"—I became aware that my prejudices had always imprisoned, never protected me.

Thus, I came to believe: That man is an impotent, confused creature, except when he develops awareness of the Supreme Being, which awareness expands into love; that power, guidance, and security come only through this love of man for God and God for man.

The universe is organized and orderly, yet every least atom is in motion. The very nature of life is movement. Consequently, there must be an organizer and a governor. When I lose my job, when my child is desperately ill, or when a friend turns against me, these incidents are not fortuitous. No, these happenings are, however painful, a significant pattern of life for me as an individual.

Once, as a child, I became tortured with the thought that my father might abandon me in a strange city. I told him. He said, "That's impossible because of love. I couldn't leave you, Rob, if I wanted to. Love is stronger than the trace chains on a twenty-mule team wagon."

Man today is like that child of fifty years ago. He is terrified that God may abandon him. But if mere man's love is as strong as steel trace chains, then God's love is unbreakable. So man—and mankind—are safe! This I believe.

ROBERT B. POWERS *entered police work after serving as a cavalry-man in World War I. He was a deputy sheriff in New Mexico and Arizona and was chief of police for Bakersfield, California. Powers co-authored* A Guide to Race Relations for Police Officers.

Nobody Can Walk the Trail Alone

LOUISE DICKINSON RICH

WHEN I WAS YOUNG, I believed that I was strong and self-sufficient. Since I was not completely stupid, I knew perfectly well with my head, if not with my heart, that life is no bed of roses. I was prepared for disappointment and for, possibly, tragedy. When they came, I'd handle them personally with style. Only sissies lean. I was afraid of nothing and I could do anything, or at least I so believed. Nothing in this world or the next could daunt me, Big Louise, the heroine.

Now I am older. I have met with poverty, flood, famine, hurricane, brutalizing labor, and illness on extremely personal grounds. I have seen the sudden and tragic deaths of those nearest and dearest to me. I have had to shoulder responsibilities, for which I am ill fitted, and the much more difficult burden of sudden, if brief, fame. I have been hard pressed for money, as we say in Maine. I'm not whining. I've had a wonderful life, with the joys far outweighing the sorrows. But still, in all, there have been times when I was fair to middlin' desperate.

There was the time when my husband and my year-old son and my mother-in-law and I had one meal a day. We ate baked potatoes and salt. It didn't do us adults any harm, and my neighbor woman, Alice Miller, provided me with six oranges and six quarts of milk a week—she kept two cows—for the baby. She said her doctor's book said that babies needed it.

Then there was the time in December. My husband and I were laughing together over a silly joke in the evening after dinner, relaxed in our slippers before the open fire. We'd spent the day snugging down the cabin for winter, and we felt good knowing that there were forty miles of lake and impossible road between us and the nearest settlement. We were having fun. "Louise, you gorgeous fool," he said, and died.

I don't know how I could possibly have survived that—because you see, I loved him from the bottom of my heart—if it hadn't been for my other neighbor, Alice Parsons. She came and sat with me, not saying a word, just with infinite wisdom being there all through the awful formalities of the coroner and the sheriff, who must investigate in Maine any case of sudden death.

There was the time after that when I owed a lot of money to a lot of people, I'm sorry to say. I went to the butcher and the baker and the candlestick maker and told them that I couldn't pay them now, but if they'd give me breathing space, I'd clear the books and, of course, pay the interest. They all gave me the same answer. "Mrs. Rich, I'm sorry to hear about your trouble. Ralph was a good man. We'll miss him a lot. About the money, take your time. I'm not worried. Anytime at your convenience, and forget the interest."

So now I have grown up. I don't believe in myself anymore, not in myself alone. I do believe in myself as a member of the human race. I believe in the decency and sympathy and kindness of every man and woman and child that I meet. Nobody, not even Big Louise, can walk the trail alone. I know that now.

I believe also that I have an obligation. Whenever I see one of my brothers or sisters in trouble—a car off the road, the need of a cup of tea in my shabby living room by the elderly lady down the road who is lonesome—I am privileged to have the opportunity to repay, in a small measure, my debt.

I don't know about God. He's too big for me to understand. But I have seen his visage reflected in the faces of the people who have helped me through my hard times. I hope to live so that someday, someone will say, "Louise Rich? Oh sure, I know her. She isn't so bad. She's human."

I believe in humanity.

LOUISE DICKINSON RICH'S *life in northern Maine became the fodder for her best-selling book,* We Took to The Woods. *Following her husband's death, Rich moved with her children back to her hometown of Bridgewater, Massachusetts, where she wrote numerous books for adults and young adults.*

Free Minds and Hearts at Work

⟋⟍

JACKIE ROBINSON

AT THE BEGINNING OF THE WORLD SERIES OF 1947, I exper-
ienced a completely new emotion when the National Anthem
was played. This time, I thought, it is being played for me, as
much as for anyone else. This is organized major league
baseball, and I am standing here with all the others, and
everything that takes place includes me.

About a year later, I went to Atlanta, Georgia, to play in
an exhibition game. On the field, for the first time in Atlanta,
there were Negroes and whites. Other Negroes, besides me.
And I thought: What I have always believed has come to be.

And what is it that I have always believed? First,
that imperfections are human. But that wherever human

beings were given room to breathe and time to think, those imperfections would disappear, no matter how slowly. I do not believe that we have found or even approached perfection. That is not necessarily in the scheme of human events. Handicaps, stumbling blocks, prejudices—all of these are imperfect. Yet, they have to be reckoned with because they are in the scheme of human events.

Whatever obstacles I found made me fight all the harder. But it would have been impossible for me to fight at all, except that I was sustained by the personal and deep-rooted belief that my fight had a chance. It had a chance because it took place in a free society. Not once was I forced to face and fight an immovable object. Not once was the situation so cast-iron rigid that I had no chance at all. Free minds and human hearts were at work all around me, and so there was the probability of improvement. I look at my children now and know that I must still prepare them to meet obstacles and prejudices.

But I can tell them, too, that they will never face some of these prejudices because other people have gone before them. And to myself I can say that, because progress is unalterable, many of today's dogmas will have vanished by the time they grow into adults. I can say to my children: There is a chance for you. No guarantee, but a chance.

And this chance has come to be, because there is nothing

static with free people. There is no Middle Ages logic so strong that it can stop the human tide from flowing forward. I do not believe that every person, in every walk of life, can succeed in spite of any handicap. That would be perfection. But I do believe—and with every fiber in me—that what I was able to attain came to be because we put behind us (no matter how slowly) the dogmas of the past: to discover the truth of today; and perhaps find the greatness of tomorrow.

I believe in the human race. I believe in the warm heart. I believe in man's integrity. I believe in the goodness of a free society. And I believe that the society can remain good only as long as we are willing to fight for it—and to fight against whatever imperfections may exist.

My fight was against the barriers that kept Negroes out of baseball. This was the area where I found imperfection, and where I was best able to fight. And I fought because I knew it was not doomed to be a losing fight. It couldn't be a losing fight—not when it took place in a free society.

And, in the largest sense, I believe that what I did was done for me—that it was my faith in God that sustained me in my fight. And that what was done for me must and will be done for others.

In 1947, JACKIE ROBINSON pioneered the integration of American professional athletics by becoming the first black player in Major League Baseball. During his ten seasons with the Brooklyn Dodgers, he played on six World Series teams and was voted the National League's Most Valuable Player in 1949.

Growth that Starts from Thinking

⁓

ELEANOR ROOSEVELT

IT SEEMS TO ME A VERY DIFFICULT THING to put into words the beliefs we hold and what they make you do in your life. I think I was fortunate because I grew up in a family where there was a very deep religious feeling. I don't think it was spoken of a great deal. It was more or less taken for granted that everybody held certain beliefs and needed certain reinforcements of their own strength and that that came through your belief in God and your knowledge of prayer.

But as I grew older I questioned a great many of the things that I knew very well my grandmother who had brought me up had taken for granted. And I think I might have been a quite difficult person to live with if it hadn't been for the fact that my husband once said it didn't do you any harm to learn those things, so why not let your children learn them? When they grow up they'll think things out for themselves.

And that gave me a feeling that perhaps that's what we all must do—think out for ourselves what we could believe and how we could live by it. And so I came to the conclusion that you had to use this life to develop the very best that you could develop.

I don't know whether I believe in a future life. I believe that all that you go through here must have some value, therefore there must be some reason. And there must be some "going on." How exactly that happens I've never been able to decide. There is a future—that I'm sure of. But how? That I don't know. And I came to feel that it didn't really matter very much because whatever the future held you'd have to face it when you came to it, just as whatever life holds you have to face it exactly the same way. And the important thing was that you never let down doing the best that you were able to do—it might be poor because you might not have very much within you to give, or to help other people with, or to live your life with. But as long as you did the very best that you were able to do, then that was what you were put here to do and that was what you were accomplishing by being here.

And so I have tried to follow that out—and not to worry about the future or what was going to happen. I think I am pretty much of a fatalist. You have to accept whatever comes and the only important thing is that you meet it with courage and with the best that you have to give.

ELEANOR ROOSEVELT, *wife of Franklin D. Roosevelt, was active in Democratic politics and helped shape her husband's New Deal programs while he was president. Considered one of the most active and influential first ladies in U.S. history, she advocated racial equality, women's rights, and world peace.*

When Children Are Wanted

Margaret Sanger

THIS I BELIEVE, first of all: that all our basic convictions must be tested and transmuted in the crucible of experience—and sometimes the more bitter the experience, the more valid the purified belief.

As a child, one of a large family, I learned that the thing I did best was the thing I liked to do. This realization of doing and getting results was what I have later called an awakening consciousness.

There is an old Indian proverb which has inspired me in the work of my adult life. "Build thou beyond thyself, but first be sure that thou thyself be strong and healthy in body and mind." Yes, to build, to work, to plan to do something, not for yourself, not for your own benefit, but "beyond thyself"—and when this idea permeates the mind you begin to think in terms of a future. I began to think of a world beyond myself when I first took an interest in nursing the sick.

As a nurse, I was in contact with the ill and the infirm. I knew something about the health and disease of bodies, but for a long time I was baffled at the tremendous personal problems of life, of marriage, of living, and of just being. Here indeed was a challenge to "build beyond thyself." But where was I to begin? I found the answer at every door. I began to believe there was something I could do toward increasing an understanding of these basic human problems. To build beyond myself I must first tap all inner resources of stamina, of courage, of resolution within myself. I was prepared to face opposition, even ridicule, denunciation. But I had also to prepare myself, in defense of these unpopular beliefs; I had to prepare myself to face courts and even prisons. But I resolved to stand up, alone if necessary, against all the entrenched forces which opposed me.

I started my battle some forty years ago. The women and mothers whom I wanted to help also wanted to help me. They, too, wanted to build beyond the self, in creating healthy children and bringing them up in life to be happy and useful citizens. I believed it was my duty to place motherhood on a higher level than enslavement and accident. I was convinced we must care about people; we must reach out to help them in their despair.

For these beliefs I was denounced, arrested. I was in and out of police courts and higher courts, and indictments hung over my life for several years. But nothing could alter my beliefs. Because I saw these as truths, and I stubbornly stuck to my convictions.

No matter what it may cost in health, in misunderstanding, in sacrifice, something had to be done, and I felt that I was called by the force of circumstance to do it. Because of my philosophy and my work, my life has been enriched and full. My interests have expanded from local conditions and needs to a world horizon, where peace on earth may be achieved when children are wanted before they are conceived. A new consciousness will take place, a new race will be born to bring peace on earth. This belief has withstood the crucible of my life's joyous struggle. It remains my basic belief today.

This I believe—at the end, as at the beginning, of my long crusade for the future of the human race.

MARGARET SANGER *was the founder and president of the American Birth Control League, which later became Planned Parenthood. She organized the first World Population Conference in Geneva in 1927. Even into her eighties, Sanger traveled the world helping establish birth control clinics.*

Finding Security In Fundamental Freedoms

MARGARET CHASE SMITH

MANY NIGHTS I GO HOME from the office or the Senate floor tired and discouraged. There's lots of glory and prestige and limelight for a United States Senator that the public sees. But there's just as much grief and harassment and discouragement that the public doesn't see.

Of course, like everyone else, I went into public service and politics with my eyes wide open. I knew that any public official is fair game for slander and smear and carping criticism. I knew that ingratitude was to be expected. I knew that fair weather friends would turn on me when they felt I no longer served their purposes. I knew that I would be called all sorts of names from crook on down. I should have known that chances were good that I would even be accused of being a traitor to my country.

These things I knew. But I never knew how vicious they could get and how deeply they could cut. It is these things I think of when I'm tired and discouraged—and when I wonder if being a Senator is worth all that I put into it. These are the times when I consider quitting public life and retreating to the comforts and luxury of private life.

But these times have always been the very times when I became all the more convinced that all the sorrow, abuse, harassment, and vilification was not too high a price or sacrifice to pay. For it is then that I ask myself, "What am I doing this for?"

I realize that I am doing it because I believe in certain things—things without which life wouldn't mean much to me.

This I do believe—that life has a real purpose: that God has assigned to each human being a role in life, that each of us has a purposeful task, that our individual roles are all different but that each of us has the same obligation to do the best we can.

I believe that every human being I come in contact with has a right to courtesy and consideration from me. I believe that I should not ask or expect from anyone else that which I am not willing to grant or do myself. I believe that I should be able to take anything that I can dish out. I believe that every living person has the right to criticize constructively, the right honestly to hold unpopular beliefs, the right to protest orderly, the right of independent thought.

I believe that no one has a right to own our souls except God.

I believe that freedom of speech should not be so abused by some that it is not exercised by others because of fear and smear. But I do believe that we should not permit tolerance to degenerate into indifference. I believe that people should never get so indifferent, cynical, and sophisticated that they don't get shocked into action.

I believe that we should not forget how to disagree agreeably and how to criticize constructively. I believe with all my heart that we must not become a nation of mental mutes blindly following demagogues. I believe that in our constant search for security we can never gain any peace of mind until we secure our own soul.

And this I do believe above all, especially in my times of greater discouragement, that I must believe—that I must believe in my fellow men, that I must believe in myself, that I must believe in God—if life is to have any meaning.

MARGARET CHASE SMITH *was a Republican Senator from Maine and was the first woman to be elected to both the United States House and the Senate. Spending four terms in the Senate and thirty-two years in Congress, she was also the first woman to be nominated for U.S. President by either of the two major parties.*

Everything Potent Is Dangerous

WALLACE STEGNER

IT IS TERRIBLY DIFFICULT to say honestly, without posing or faking, what one truly and fundamentally believes. Reticence or an itch to make public confession may distort or dramatize what is really there to be said, and public expressions of belief are so closely associated with inspirational activity and, in fact, so often stem from someone's desire to buck up the downhearted and raise the general morale, that belief becomes an evangelical matter.

In all honesty, what I believe is neither inspirational nor evangelical. Passionate faith I am suspicious of because it hangs witches and burns heretics, and generally I am more in sympathy with the witches and heretics than with the sectarians who hang and burn them. I fear immoderate zeal, Christian, Moslem, Communist, or whatever, because it restricts the range of human understanding and the wise reconciliation of human differences, and creates an orthodoxy with a sword in its hand.

I cannot say that I am even a sound Christian, though the code of conduct to which I subscribe was preached more eloquently by Jesus Christ than by any other. About God I simply do not know; I don't think I can know.

However far I have missed achieving it, I know that moderation is one of the virtues I most believe in. But I believe as well in a whole catalogue of Christian and classical virtues: in kindness and generosity, in steadfastness and courage, and much else. I believe further that good depends not on things but on the use we make of things. Everything potent, from human love to atomic energy, is dangerous; it produces ill about as readily as good; it becomes good only through the control, the discipline, the wisdom with which we use it. Much of this control is social, a thing which laws and institutions and uniforms enforce, but much of it must be personal, and I do not see how we can evade the obligation to take full responsibility for what we individually do. Our reward for self-control and the acceptance of private responsibility is not necessarily money or power. Self-respect and the respect of others are quite enough.

All this is to say that I believe in conscience, not as something implanted by divine act, but as something learned from infancy from the tradition and society which has bred us. The outward forms of virtue will vary greatly from nation to nation; a Chinese scholar of the old school, or an Indian raised on the Vedas and the Bhagavad Gita, has a conscience that will differ from mine. But in the essential outlines of what constitutes human decency we vary amazingly little. The Chinese and the Indian know as well as I do what kindness is, what generosity is, what fortitude is. They can define justice quite as accurately. It is only when they and I are blinded by tribal and denominational narrowness that we insist upon our differences and can recognize goodness only in the robes of our own crowd.

Man is a great enough creature and a great enough enigma to deserve both our pride and our compassion, and engage our fullest sense of mystery. I shall certainly never do as much with my life as I want to, and I shall sometimes fail miserably to live up to my conscience, whose word I do not distrust even when I can't obey it. But I am terribly glad to be alive; and when I have wit enough to think about it, terribly proud to be a man and an American, with all the rights and privileges that those words connote; and most of all I am humble before the responsibilities that are also mine. For no right comes without a responsibility, and being born luckier than most of the world's millions, I am also born more obligated.

Writer and educator WALLACE STEGNER *published over thirty novels, collections of short stories and essays, and historical works.* The Big Rock Candy Mountain *was among his most popular novels, and* Angle of Repose *won the 1972 Pulitzer Prize for Fiction. Stegner wrote about the American West, which he also fought to protect.*

The Birthright of Human Dignity

⌒

WILL THOMAS

In 1946, I decided I did not wish to live in my native land any longer; and that I would take my wife and children to Haiti, where as Negroes in a Negro republic, we would be free of racial prejudice and our opportunities would be limited only by our ability to use them.

I do not believe I need detail the reasons behind this unhappy decision, except to say that being considered and treated as an inferior on every level of life can become intolerable, especially when it is by one's race rather than his individual worth, or lack of it, that he is pre-judged—and condemned.

When I reached this point, I had become an unbeliever

in both God and country, for it seemed to me that racial segregation and all that it implied was as rigid on the spiritual as
on the temporal plane. And so finally I made the decision to
leave my native land—permanently.

However, I did not do it. Love of country, I found, can
be very deep, very strong. So I thought to make one final try
in my motherland for the equality of status which I considered I had been denied; and I chose Vermont for the experiment. I reasoned that because of its great traditions of
personal freedom there was at least a chance that I and my
family might find there what we so yearned for, and we did.
In the small farming community where we settled, we were
accepted on a basis of individuality unqualified by race.

However, it is not that which now seems most important
to me. It is, rather, that in such a friendly atmosphere, and
amid the quiet of a beautiful countryside, it was possible to
think calmly and gradually to gain understandings by which
I believe I can live in peace with other men, and with myself,
for the rest of my life.

One of these understandings is that unless one seeks
sincerely for whatever it is he most wants, he surely will not
find it, and that what I really had been seeking most of my
life was not what I wanted but instead was justification for
the resentments I felt. This is not to say there was not cause
for those resentments, but rather that I had so concentrated

upon them I could not see that the picture was not all bad—
that, in fact, there was considerable good in it.

I had condemned my country and my religion because I
viewed only what seemed wrong in both. But when I was able
to remove the blinds of my own prejudice, it became clear that
these failures, these flaws in church and state, were human
failures, human flaws, and not mere self-willed bigotry; and
that within each there were, and there always had been, many
who had worked and fought for what was right.

I think the core of my earlier bitterness had been the
conviction that I had been denied my birthright of human
dignity. But I know now that is something which cannot be
given or taken away by man.

It has been written that he who seeks shall find, and that
to him who asks, it shall be given. And I can only testify that
when I did seek, I did find; and that when I asked, it was
given to me. And I know that only the God I once denied
could bestow such precious gifts.

WILL THOMAS *was born in Kansas City and worked as a newspaper writer, editor, and prizefighter. He eventually settled in Vermont with his wife and three children. His book,* The Seeking, *details the family's integration into the all-white community of Westford.*

A Public Man

—

HARRY S. TRUMAN

I BELIEVE IN A MORAL CODE based on the Ten Commandments found in the twentieth Chapter of Exodus, and in the fifth, sixth, and seventh Chapters of the Gospel according to St. Matthew, which is the Sermon on the Mount.

I believe a man ought to live by those precepts, which, if followed, will enable a man to do right.

I don't know whether I have or not, but I have tried.

I believe that the fundamental basis for a happy life with family and friends is to treat others as you would like to be treated, speak truthfully, act honorably, and keep commitments to the letter.

In public life I have always believed that right will prevail.

It has been my policy to obtain the facts—all the facts possible—then to make the decision in the public interest and to carry it out.

If the facts justify the decision at the time it is made, it will always be right. A public man should not worry constantly about the verdict of history or what future generations will say about him.

He must live in the present, make his decisions for the right on the facts as he sees them and history will take care of itself.

I believe a public man must know the history and background of his state and his nation to enable him to come more nearly to a proper decision in the public interest.

In my opinion, a man in public life must think always of the public welfare. He must be careful not to mix his private and personal interests with his public actions.

The ethics of a public man must be unimpeachable.

He must learn to reject unwise or imprudent requests from friends and associates without losing their friendship or loyalty.

I believe that our Bill of Rights must be implemented in fact, that it is the duty of every Government—state, local, or federal—to preserve the rights of the individual.

I believe that a civil rights program, as we must practice it today, involves not so much the protection of the people against the government, but the protection of the people by the government. And for this reason, we must make the federal government a friendly, vigilant defender of the rights and equalities of all Americans, and that every man should be free to live his life as he wishes. He should be limited only by his responsibility to his fellow man.

I believe that we should remove the last barriers which stand between millions of our people and their birthright. There can be no justifiable reason for discrimination because of ancestry, or religion, or race, or color.

I believe that to inspire the people of the world whose freedom is in jeopardy, and to restore hope to those who have already lost their civil liberties, we must correct the remaining imperfections in our own democracy.

We know the way—we only need the will.

HARRY S. TRUMAN *was the thirty-third President of the United States, serving from 1945 to 1953. Born and raised in Missouri, Truman was a farmer, businessman, World War I veteran, and U.S. Senator. As president, his order to drop atomic bombs on Japan helped end World War II.*

A Twinge of Conscience

PETER USTINOV

I MUST ADMIT AT ONCE that I am one of those people who reach their conclusions about faith by a process of elimination rather than as a result of an opening of private heavens. I am aware that there are conventions which believe faith to be as blind and beautiful as love, and even if I cannot subscribe to this, I feel that people like myself, even if incapable of mystical frenzies, have the consolation of being far less dangerous to our fellow-men.

Organized religion as such depresses me, in that I can never accept the idea of the church as an agency of God, with different denominations as active in claiming the attention of the layman as are those corporations who jockey for position in the world of commerce. When this practice of agency reaches the pitch of deciding a child's religion before it is born, I rebel, or rather, my conscience rebels. Parenthood is not a selfish investment. It is a happy accident by which human beings can perform the miracle of creating a character, a conscience, and a mind, the whole served up with identifiable features. I believe that the parents' function is to allow the young mind full rein, so that it may grow up with the dignity of doubt rather than with the servility of imposed convictions.

I resent attempts at conversion by any slave to a sense of mission, be he political or divine. I have nothing against the hermetic mind so long as it is not allied to a moralizing mouth. My grandfather, whom I never knew, was converted from Orthodoxy to Protestantism. I believe that had he not done so, I might easily have taken the same step, although, as I said, I find the habit of religion oppressive, and an easy way out of personal thought. It is, in any case, a temperamental difference in the believers which separates the churches, and not a religious difference. If I can't put up with the interfering dogmas, I am prepared and proud to be called a Christian, because it is a convenient and beautiful adjective with which to label the grain of virtue latent in the human conscience.

I believe in doubt and mistrust conviction; I believe in liberalism and detest oppression; I believe in the individual and deny the existence of the so-called masses; I believe in abstract love of country and deplore patriotism; I believe in moral courage and suspect physical courage for its own sake; I believe in the human conscience and deny the right of fanatics or of those with self-created haloes to impinge on its necessary privacy.

The mysticism of mortals is an attempt to colonize obscurity for the purpose of religious oppression, while a twinge of conscience is a glimpse of God.

SIR PETER USTINOV *was a prolific actor, director, writer, and journalist, appearing in more than one-hundred film and television productions. He wrote and directed many acclaimed stage plays and led numerous international theatrical productions. Ustinov was the winner of numerous awards over his life, including two Academy Awards, three Emmys, one Grammy, and a Golden Globe.*

Goodness Doesn't Just Happen

~~

Rebecca West

I BELIEVE IN LIBERTY. I feel it is necessary for the health of the world that every man shall be able to say and do what he wishes and what is within his power, for each human being has a unique contribution to make toward our understanding of life, because every man is himself unique. His physical and his mental makeup is unique, and his circumstances are unique. So he must be able to tell us something which could not be learned from any other source.

I wish I believed this only when I am writing about politics, but I believe it also in my capacity as a woman with a family and friends. I don't find it makes life easy. It happens that if you let a man say and do what he likes, there comes a point when he wants to say or do something which interferes with the liberty of someone else to say or do what he likes.

Therefore, it follows that I see as the main problem of my life, the balancing of competitive freedoms. This involves a series of very delicate calculations, and you can never stop making them. This principle has to be applied in personal relations, and everybody knows that the Ready Reckoner to use there is love, but it takes a lot of real talent to use love effectively. The principle has to be applied in social relations also, and there the Ready Reckoner is the Rule of Law, political scientists call it, a sense of mutual obligations that have to be honored and a legal system which can be trusted to step in when that sense fails.

When I was young, I understood neither the difficulty of love nor the importance of law. I grew up in a world of rebellion, and I was a rebel. I thought human beings were naturally good, and that their personal relations were bound to work out well, and that the law was a clumsy machine dealing harshly with people who would cease to offend as soon as we got rid of poverty. And we were all quite sure that human nature would soon be perfect.

Yes, I can remember that when I was something like eleven years old, a visitor to my mother's home who had been in Russia described how she had one day been caught in the middle of a pogrom, and had seen the Cossacks knouting

6915414R0

Made in the USA
Charleston, SC
23 December 2010